MUSKEG, MOSQUITOES AND MOOSE

Meet the Author

Joyce Allene Stone grew up in Brazil, Indiana, where she lived until teaching opportunities took her to southern Indiana. For the past sixteen years she has taught special education in the learning disabilities area. Prior to that she taught English and music for thirteen years.

Joyce and her husband have been canoe camping since 1980. Their first major camping venture was in the Boundary Waters Canoe Area. More recently, Fred and Joyce have gone to solo canoes, spending several summer vacations paddling Quetico-Superior Provincial Park.

*Oh Boy!*_____

MUSKEG, MOSQUITOES AND MOOSE

_____*It Just Doesn't Get Any Better Than This!*

By

Joyce Allene Stone

Library of Congress Catalog Card Number: 91-51232

ISBN: 0-923568-25-5

Typesetting: Boufford Typesetters

Cover photograph: Joyce Allene Stone

Cartography: Marjorie Nash Klein

Line drawings: June Porter

Library of Congress Cataloging-in-Publication Data

Stone, Joyce Allene, 1939 –
    Oh boy! muskeg, mosquitoes, and moose : it just doesn't get any better than this / Joyce Allene Stone.
       p.   cm.
  ISBN 0-923568-25-5 (pbk.)
    1. Northwest, Canadian—Description and travel—1981 – 2. Canoes and canoeing—Canada, Northwest. I. Title. II. Title: Muskeg, mosquitoes, and moose.
F1060.92.S76 1992
917.12—dc20   91-51232
                                     CIP

Published by Wilderness Adventure Books
Fowlerville, Michigan 48864

Manufactured in the United States of America

To my hero

Contents

Contents

WHAT IT'S ABOUT

This book is not a history
Or facts about geography.
'Cause accurate, those books must be,
And that's for experts, not for me.

This is a simple tale I told
Of how I felt when once cajoled
By Fred, my mate, with heart of gold,
To make a trip like men of old.

My heart and soul were wracked with doubt
When we discussed this fearsome route.
I wasn't bold or brave or stout;
Should I go with him or back out?

We left to go into the sticks,
Both forty-five and out for kicks.
We knew we'd have to take some licks;
I prayed I'd reach age forty-six!

Just In Case

"In case something happens to us. . . ."

"In case we don't come back. . . ."

"Be sure to take care of ___ just in case. . . ."

I wore these phrases thin while my husband and I were making plans for this outrageous trip he had talked me into. How could we possibly paddle a canoe more than 600 miles through the North Country? A teacher and a truck driver—alone! Together! Could we stand being away from civilization for a month and a half? What were the worst possible things that could happen to us?

An eight-hundred-pound polar bear shredding me into bite-sized pieces was in first place. The canoe plunging over a falls shredding me into bite-sized pieces ranked second. Running a close third was the fear that something would happen to my husband. That "something," I had speculated, would undoubtedly disable Fred to the degree that he would have to depend on me to save his life. Or worse, he might even be injured so badly that he would recite those old thriller movie lines: "I can't make it. Save yourself! Go on without me!" I had visions of myself dragging the canoe across portages or trying to fire the shotgun at a charging bear. Then, never daring to dream that I would be able to handle the stern, I would get into the bow of the canoe and paddle around lost on a huge lake until I starved to death or until five-foot waves swamped me or bashed the canoe to pieces on a rocky shoreline.

I wearied myself making plans to prevent such tragedies. Good sense and careful timing would ward off most of them, I knew. It was the possibility of plain old bad luck that kept me working at getting my earthly possessions in order, making our will, and writing page after page of directions to our children on "what to do if. . . ." At Corydon Elementary School where I teach learning disabled children, my friends were beginning to respond to my predictions of doom with frustrated shouts of, "Joyce! Will you cut that out! You're going to come BACK!"

I had taken a course in CPR and knew that the first thing I was supposed to say to the victim was, "Can you speak?" I figured Fred would always be able to speak unless he were thoroughly dead, so I didn't worry much about the rest of the instructions. I carried a small booklet of survival tips and a Swiss army knife with a variety of important emergency tools, such as a corkscrew, a toothpick, and a nail cleaner. I also carried a whistle, a small canister of mace, and three sizeable swatches of fluorescent nylon cloth to signal small planes flying over, just in case. . . .

For several years, Fred had been driving a semi-tractor-trailer over the road for a freight company. I believed him when he said, "The highway going to the North Country is more dangerous than any river we're going to paddle after we get there." But I rejected his philosophy on wild bears. "They're more afraid of you than you are of them," he said. *NO WAY!* Even the Eskimos had great respect for Nanook. I also intended to respect them—from as far away as possible.

So while Fred was telling our friends about the exciting Hayes River trip and how we would paddle right out on Hudson Bay, I was smiling lamely in the background, trying my best to look confident. Our friends' eyes would widen at his descriptions of how remote the area was and how many days we were likely to be "out." Then these motel vacationers, whose idea of roughing it is to do without cable TV, would look at me as if to say, *You're going with this lunatic to a place where you can't even take a hot bath every day!* I would meet their glances proudly and say, "That country is beautiful. We'll show you our slides if . . . I mean, *when* we get back."

They would look at Fred and say polite things like, "Gee, I bet that'll be fun. I can't wait to hear all about it if . . . I mean, *when* you get back." At least one or two of those with whom we shared our insanity had the decency to say, "I envy you. I wish I had the time off from work to do something like that." We both knew they were secretly relieved that they would never have that much time off, even after they retired. Fred's main reason for wanting to make this particular trip was to follow the route the fur traders and trappers had used during the eighteenth and nineteenth centuries. But when he would explain to these fascinated listeners that our destination was an abandoned fur factory started by the Hudson's Bay Company in 1682, they struggled to maintain the spell-bound look while they covertly glanced at their watches.

Actually, we were both very serious about becoming involved in the historic aspect of the trip. Our departure point was to be the Cree Indian reserve, Cumberland House, Saskatchewan. Samuel Hearne had started the first inland trading post there for Hudson's Bay Company in

1774. Being ridiculously tender-hearted toward animals, I had to avoid concentrating on the large numbers that were killed during this important era in Canadian history. I keep trying to believe there might have been a few other reasons besides the lust for furs that the beautiful North Country was explored and settled. But I had to come to terms with the fact that the fur trade was responsible for most of the settlements which lined the main routes of travel.

We just didn't have the time nor the strength to do everything the old way. It would have been fun to wear the voyageur's costume—tasseled stocking cap, short shirt, leggings held up by a string tied to a belt around the waist, deerskin moccasins, and a colorful wide sash with a pouch hanging from it. When I thought about my light-weight rain gear, however, I decided that my personal desire to remain unsaturated transcended the possible manifestation of pleasure from the imitation of traditional costume. In other words, it ain't no fun to be cold and wet, no matter how cute you look! And, I was willing to carry heavy loads, but the two ninety-pound packs the voyageurs wore while they trotted across the trails seemed a bit much for my hundred-and-twenty-pound frame.

The tripmen weren't very big either, though. They averaged about five feet, six inches. Long-legged men would have taken too much precious storage room in the canoes. The tripmen were said to have been stocky and muscular in the arms and shoulders. They undoubtedly acquired the Popeye physique from the fifteen-hour days they put in behind the paddle. They had to have sturdy legs for portaging, too. The voyageurs were highly competitive in both canoe and dog-sled travel. It was disgraceful to admit fatigue or even frostbite. Their strength of mind evidently outweighed their strength of body. Many of them were

crippled by the time they reached middle age. What we
had read about the voyageurs led us to imagine them
cursing at foul weather and swarms of insects, singing to
the stroke of the paddle, and laughing with anticipation of
the revelry at journey's end.

"Bannock and beans" strikes the ear pleasantly
enough. I'm sure the famished tripman couldn't wait to
break off a hunk of the bread and dip it in his bowl. The
bannock I produced in a practice session at home was
hard, tasteless, and ugly. Maybe I wasn't hungry enough
to appreciate it. I decided to stick to pancakes. At least I'm
able to recognize failure in a flapjack. Of course, "freeze-
dried food" also had a nice ring to it.

We thought we would never be ready to leave home.
Actually, we never were quite ready, but we left anyhow,
finally. The car was full of camping gear and luggage. We
hadn't been able to squeeze in the wood-burning stove or
the piano because the kitchen sink took up too much
room. Really we had tried to pack quite prudently. We left
so many things out of our gear because of weight, that we
just hoped we had everything we *needed*. Would forty-five
rolls of thirty-six-exposure film be enough? We had packed
the elastic knee bandage and ankle wrap; they were neces-
sities, we had learned. I had tucked packages of waterproof
matches in several different bags so that if one bag were
lost in a rapids, we would still have hopes of keeping warm
and cooking food, should there be any food left to cook. A
length of 20-gauge wire and even wire cutters had been
desperately needed on a couple of other trips, so we knew
we couldn't do without them on this one. At last, we lifted
the *Hoosier Transit* onto the canoe racks, and Fred cinched
it so tightly to the ends of the bumpers that I was afraid the
car would begin to "smile." In spite of the fact that I had
checked off all of the items on my dozen or so dog-eared

lists, I was sure I had forgotten one or two serious respon-
sibilities, neglected a couple of life-threatening details, or at
least overlooked a devastating financial obligation. It made
me sad to say good-bye to Ralph and Pearl, our two
Siberian Huskies; Mollie, the black mutt; and Bonnie, the
"fatted cat." I hoped that, if something happened to us. . . .
"Let go of it!" I told myself. We walked out of the house,
got in the car, and broke free!

PRE-PARTUM PARENTS

Goodbye, and be good;
　We do love you all.
If we make York Factory,
　We'll give you a call.

Take care of the cat,
　And don't spoil the dogs.
Ration their food,
　'Cause they eat like hogs.

If something should happen
　That we don't get back,
You'll find the house key
　On a nail out back.

Let *NO ONE* come in!
　Just set it on fire.
My housekeeping habits
　Leave much to desire!

If we don't see you
　Again on this earth,
Take care of yourselves;
　Do something "of worth."

If we would get lost,
　After all this fuss,
Think who'd last longest:
　YOU? or *US?*

Arriving At The Departure Point

Two days of hard driving took us from Southern Indiana to The Pas, a town on the western edge of central Manitoba. That part of the trip, however, was reduced to leisurely vacation travel when it was later compared with the four-and-a-half-hour journey from The Pas to Cumberland House, Saskatchewan.

We started from The Pas at 6:30 A.M. in order to make our put-in before noon. Those 165 miles gave us an entirely new perspective on other people's definitions of the word "road." The thousands of tiny hills and valleys on the mushy surface of gravel, clay, and "quicksand" were laughingly called *bumps* by folks in those parts. Little yellow signs with black jagged lines were cues for the driver to prepare for anything from skittering across a washboard road to catapulting across the Canadian Grand Canyon.

The only human life existing on that part of the planet

was in the form of a couple of small work crews operating dozers and road graders. By all outward appearances, their purpose in life was to keep the road mildly passable. I suspected they might have been ambassadors from Canada's Department of Tourism, periodically stationed along the highways to convince lonely motorists that the road had not ended.

To top it all off, we hadn't eaten breakfast, thinking we'd grab something at one of the gasoline stations. We figured there would be two or three of these along the way and they surely would be like the ones we'd seen in other sparsely-populated parts of the North Country, a combination of filling station, cafe, and grocery store. The *one* we finally came to, about two hours out, was not like that at all. It was closed! In spite of feeling as if we might starve and be picked clean by buzzards, we knew our weakened bodies would revive quickly after food was administered. The car's hunger was another matter. It would have to run on fumes for the remainder of the drive. So the shortage of food and gasoline magnified the stress brought on by bouncing and jostling along the cavernous road during the final two hours.

We had no idea what to expect at Cumberland House. The faces were mostly Indian, and the voice inflections had the Northern lilt with phrases of Cree mixed in. The buildings were simple and inexpensively built. In general, the settlement met the criteria for a small town. It had come a long way since Sam and the boys had camped out there 211 years before. Hearne and his crew of eight white men and two Indians would be interested in the appearance of the town they had founded. An annual celebration of that event was to take place a few days after our arrival. Samuel Hearne Days were celebrated with canoe races, backpacking contests, and even three-day races that involved ca-

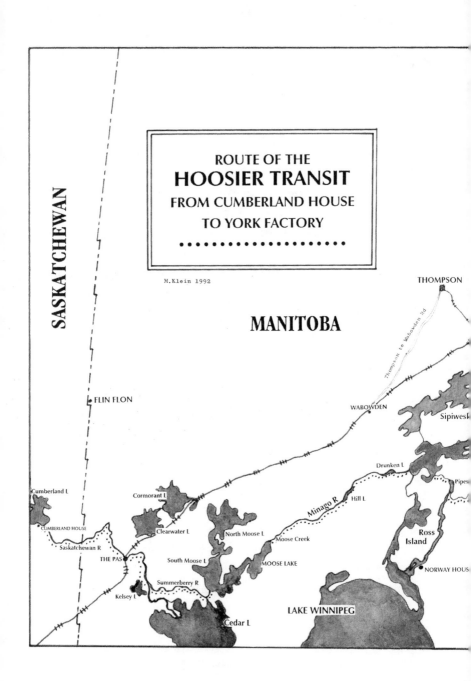

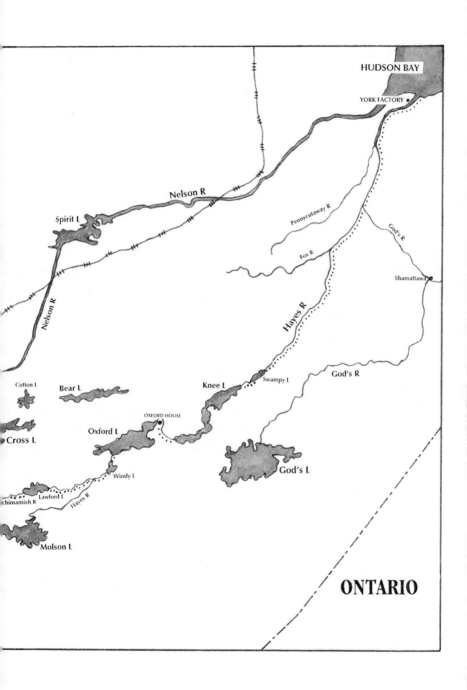

noeing, camping, and portaging over several miles of wilderness.

At the sight of the first gasoline station, the car lunged at the pump and drank its fill. When we began hunting a place to buy our late breakfast, people steered us to a small hotel in which there was a dining area. We sat down in it, hoping someone would find us and bring us nourishment before it was too late. There was very little movement, and we began to think no one was awake yet. Then a man we thought must be Chinese came out to take our order. His reply to Fred's inquiry about a cup of coffee was, "It's over there." He jerked his thumb back over his shoulder toward a coffee pot and cups. At that time, we hadn't been in enough small restaurants in the North Country to realize that pouring coffee is the responsibility of the coffee drinker, not the coffee maker. The customer is simply trusted to serve himself the number of cups and refills allowed by the prices on the menu. Our waiter seemed to feel that giving information about the food they served was almost beneath his dignity. We ordered eggs "over easy" and toast. Fred nearly jeopardized our whole meal by asking for fried potatoes. "Naw!" the man snarled, "we don't have any." I was afraid he was going to ask us to leave. He could afford to be rude. There were no golden arches within 500 miles.

When we felt our strength returning, we made contact with Marguerite Allard, wife of Bill Allard, the man who was going to fly out to Cumberland House and drive our car back to The Pas. He would park it in his yard until we returned after The Trip. We would be setting a new personal record in length of shuttle service.

By 11:30 A.M., we felt as if we had done a hard day's work. We made a few inquiries about the set of rapids we would encounter on the Saskatchewan River within about

"Where did we go wrong! We've gotta put all that stuff in the canoe and paddle it across a whole province, not to mention carrying it part of the time!"

seven miles. Then we found our put-in on Big Stone Creek and unloaded the car. I perched on the edge of the canoe and looked around me. We would have to carry all that stuff over portages. Tons of it! On our backs! I remembered how hard we had worked to select only the bare-bones items and how we had struggled until we got the total weight down to 234 pounds. But there it was heaped around us, the smallest, the lightest, and the least of what we needed merely to survive the wilderness. Surely the old fur traders and tripmen had a better system than that! Well, two cameras might seem a bit redundant, but when we each have one, we avoid long "discussions" about the many once-in-a-lifetime shots that were missed because the other one had the camera.

So, I thought, *this is The Big Moment: Two worn-out people heaving water-proof bags into the canoe. Isn't anyone else going to notice? Doesn't anyone care that we are embarking on THE ADVENTURE OF OUR LIVES!* We set the auto-timer on the camera and took our own departure picture.

We inserted the gear into the canoe, tied it all down, and by some miracle (and Fred's careful planning for every available inch of space), we found just enough room left for each of us to get in. And we'd even remembered to bring the paddles, unlike another time when we had climbed into the canoe on a lake in Indiana fifty miles from home; Fred had assumed I'd brought the paddles, and I had assumed . . . . But that's another story, an excellent illustration of the trials and tribulations our marriage has had to surmount. We shoved away from the dock, our car, our food sources, our family, friends, and home. As we drew away from all telephones, I wondered if I'd told the kids the number of the man who roots out the sewer when the toilet backs up in the basement.

WE'RE OFF!

The bands played,
The crowds cheered,
The mayor wished us well.

We smiled and bowed,
Waved and nodded;
They tolled the old church bell.

Banners and ribbons,
Balloons and flags,
Were bright in the morning air.

Dignitaries
And common folk
A bon voyage did share.

"Succeed!" they said.
"Your fame will live.
You'll have your place in the sun!"

"It is," they said,
"The noblest thing
A man and wife have done."

So filled with joy
And confidence,
I stood in silent bliss.

But suddenly,
My body lurched!
Something was amiss!

The crowds were gone,
The songs had ceased;
All was grubby and gray.

I had awakened
In our front seat
Of the Buick, still on its way.

We finally arrived
At the put-in point,
Alone, just Fred and I.

Nobody there
To wish us well,
Or even to wave good-bye.

We paddled away
On our Big Trip.
Would we ever return?

It didn't matter
To any, save us;
The victory was ours to earn.

We were the ones
Who'd feel the pride
And triumph over pain.

No one else
Would ever go
With us through wind and rain.

We would come back,
Better by far,
For all the trouble and strife.

There would be nothing
We couldn't do;
We'd have a new grip on life.

We pulled away
From the dock alone;
The world knew nothing of it.

But I heard horns
And bells and whistles;
At last, I began to love it!

Finally Underway

It was only a short distance to the first set of rapids—*too* short for my taste. In my fear-warped opinion, they seemed swollen and abnormally loud. We had asked a few people back at Cumberland House about them. A couple had told us it would be easy to canoe through the riffle. The motor-boaters had said, "I sure wouldn't try it in a canoe!" Others had smiled vaguely and said, "River's up!" I had been influenced by the negative comments. Fred had been influenced very little at all. I am a shining example of the *un*bold and the *un*brave in this world. I have always felt that anticipating disaster will help me prepare for it. In reality, this anticipation only forces me to suffer vicariously from disasters which never occur. Shakespeare knew me pretty well—"Cowards die many times before their deaths . . . ."

After an evaluation of the various opinions and advice, we had come up with exactly the same amount of insight into the situation as when we had looked at the topographical maps spread out on our living room floor. Based on the fact that the canoe was loaded down with every possession we needed in order to make the trip last longer than the current forty-five minutes, we concluded that carrying the gear around the bit of rough water seemed the wise thing to do.

The decision to carry around was so easy; the actual portage, so difficult. The riverbank offered very little footing on its steep muddy slope strewn with ankle-breaking boulders. Even Fred-be-nimble, who can usually balance on a pebble in the middle of a roaring stream, slipped one leg into the river. I carried a few small things, but in addition to being unbold and unbrave, I am also unbalanced, *mostly* in the physical sense. I was virtually helpless on that terrain.

At the conclusion of all the slipping and sliding, we faced the rapids with an empty canoe, bobbing on the water like an eggshell, and Fred's enthusiasm, a little damp around the edges, but strong as ever. "Listen," Fred said, "it's going to be next to impossible to carry the canoe across that rocky slope. We'll just run the rapids with it empty!"

I was still scanning my brain for the most effective choice of words with which to express my opposition to going through the rapids empty or otherwise, when I found myself climbing into the canoe. My subconscious mind had already realized the futility of trying to dissuade my strong-willed partner. Another reason I made myself get into the canoe was related to the small guilt trip I was experiencing. I had held my breath every time Fred's foot slipped on a boulder, thinking that at any moment he might break an ankle under the weight of his enormous packs. I didn't want to watch him carry the canoe across, too. I was afraid the strain might be too much for me! So with my teeth clenched and my paddle in the vise-grip of my fingers, I prepared to follow through on that part of the old-fashioned marriage vow which implied that I should obey this man, who had likewise vowed to love and protect me.

We dug in. The current swept us down into the rapids. We slid down a small trough or two, through some semi-bumpy standing waves, and, with the exception of a slight wobble or two in the roughest water, sailed through it so easily that I wondered why I had ever been concerned.

We swung into the bank to pick up our portaged gear and then headed on down the Saskatchewan River. It has a decent current, carrying quite a volume of water for its approximate three-hundred-foot width. It was one of the main rivers used by the fur traders in the eighteenth century.

We hadn't planned to paddle a great distance our first day out, so when a large gravel bar offered itself as a campsite, we jumped on it. It was a pleasant place. The only slightly negative features were the usual herd of mosquitoes and a few lumps under the tent.

My duties have always included building the fire and cooking the meals. That evening, I was my own worst enemy when I began battling the awkwardness and absentmindedness that had set in during the eleven months since I had last performed those rites. My memory of where things had been put in the packs, my sequence of motions, and my working rhythm all needed vast improvement. In other words: hunt and fumble, drop and retrieve, hurry and wait. I tried to conceal my mini-disasters and feign some semblance of organization in front of my mate, who was beginning to lose that tolerant "I'm-not-really-hungry-yet-anyhow" look.

A merciful distraction appeared in the form of a couple of fishermen who brought their motorboat over to the bank near our campsite. As we exchanged greetings, the two young Cree Indians hopped out of their boat and came up to where we were. Fred, with typical rural Southern Indiana hospitality, offered them some coffee, which fortunately was the one thing I had managed to get underway at that point in my camping career. They sat down on a rock slab and chatted for awhile, telling us that they were cousins and their names were Kevin Greenleaf and Ken Dolan. They had fishing nets staked out in several places along the river and were checking them for the day's catch. They soon went on their way, offering to stop back later and take us to see a sturgeon, a fish not usually found in our own local waters. We were interested but really tired. After I finally resurrected some freeze-dried food, we ate and were asleep by the time darkness had fallen.

The next day began with "rosy fingers," but both the weather and our luck at finding campsites turned on us during the longest continuous period of time we had spent paddling, ever! The muddy riverbanks, perpendicular to the water and thick with saplings and bushes, hadn't even afforded so much as a stepping-out place. Talk about control of bodily functions!

And then, we paddled right off the charts. We hadn't even purchased the next map because all it showed was a small bend in the river that went right back onto the following map. The plan had sounded simple enough to execute, but we hadn't taken into consideration that it was the first time we had even been around that particular bend. There were no familiar landmarks or land formations by which to gauge our progress. We could determine the directions by using a compass, and we could estimate the mileage by checking our watches. Where the rub came in was deciding exactly at what point, in all that look-alike scenery, we were actually going to be entering the area shown on the next map. Even when we had paddled so long that we felt sure we must be back on the map, we still couldn't identify our exact location. We were stuck in limbo. Those ambiguous miles strained our paddling arms, our backs, and our dispositions.

Harvey Anderson was the Regional Superintendent of Engineering and Construction for the Manitoba Department of Natural Resources at The Pas. He was a really nice man. A couple of his pet phrases, however, haunted us for many weary miles. When I had asked where we would be allowed to camp along the Saskatchewan and Summerberry rivers, he said, "Oh, you can camp anywhere along the banks. No problem! No sweat!" He looked at the map as Fred traced our prospective route. I think he even used those phrases about some of the portages we would be making. On several occasions, as we were living out the map dream, we wondered what No-sweat Harvey would say about some of our problems. Several times, I made mental notes to tell Mr. Anderson that, though he had been very helpful on all other counts, he was definitely wrong about the sweat. There was lots of it.

After thirteen hours, we were grateful to find an area cleared enough to put a tent down. It had been gouged out of the mud and rocks by heavy equipment for a new wildlife preserve under construction by an organization called Ducks Unlimited.

Erecting a tent after sundown in the North Country is *THE PITS!* Dusk is the mosquitoes' finest hour. Somehow we pulled it off, but because both of us were exhausted to the very edge of our patience and good humor, the usual setting-up-camp reparté was laced with snappishness and hostility.

"Get out my flashlight," Fred said. "We're going to need it in just a few minutes."

"Where is it?"

"In my belt pack, where it *always* is." He let eight seconds drift by before he said, "Haven't you got that flashlight yet?"

"It's not in your pack. I'm hunting for my pack now."

After another twenty seconds, Fred said, "Do we even still *own* a flashlight of any kind?"

"*YES, YES, YES!* I can't even find my belt pack. If you'd let me handle *my* stuff and you'd take care of your *own*, I'd know where it is!"

And so on, until, miraculously, both bodies were zipped in the tent, safe from the droning hoards "without." Supper consisted of granola bars. We ran a brief field test on the effects of granola crumbs against bare skin inside a sleeping bag. The results indicated that they possess abrasive properties strong enough to remove paint from battleships. Dessert was a couple of cookies left over from civilization a day and a half before.

"Where's the water bottle?" from my partner.

Silence, from me.

"You left it *outside?*"

Continued silence.

"You left it outside, *IN THE PACK?*"

Halfway through that emotion-packed query, I had begun putting on my shoes with as much haste as the tired old bones could muster. The water was important because both of us had sweat a great deal, contrary to Harvey's promise, and we needed to replace the loss. Besides, it is a real challenge, though not impossible, to swallow aspirins dry. I unzipped and rezipped the tent behind me with lightning speed so that only three or four of the little droners were clever enough to slip through security to the banquet inside. I ran the thirty-foot gauntlet to the backpack. The stubborn fasteners yielded grudgingly under my attack, and the trophy was mine. I made the return trip in record time. The deed was done. I had donated a pint of blood, but the cause, I rationalized, was a good one: the rebirth of peace and civility in the camp. We had just enough strength left for a long drink of water and an exchange of fond good-nights.

DINNER IS SERVED

Now where's that silly salt?
I thought I put it here!
My spoon is gone,
I laid it on
That rock behind the gear.

I need more sticks to burn
To get the water hot.
The wood is damp
Around this camp,
A roaring fire, it's not!

I thought I packed the plates
With all the cooking stuff.
Can't find a knife
To save my life.
This meal is getting tough!

Where has the small blue bag
Of instant coffee gone?
It *must* be here!
If not, I fear
This meal cannot go on!

The fire! At last, it burns!
Of course, there's too much flame.
The skillet sizzles,
Now rain drizzles.
Black flies take their aim.

Don't ask me, "What is this?"
Just eat it and be quick.
You should be glad
Some food you've had.
(Please, God, he *can't* be sick!)

Passing The Pas

The next morning, before we had moved enough to realize we didn't ever want to move again, we felt good about being within a couple of hours of The Pas. We were out on the river in a hurry, and with the current pushing us, we made good time in spite of tender backs and arms.

We saw two deer in the distance and floated as close as we could before they caught wind of us and panicked. Scrambling among the samplings on the steep bank for a hundred yards or so, they tried to find a way to get up the side of it. The larger one crashed through and made it over the top, but the smaller one clambered along the bank until it slipped into a washed-out spot and fell down into the water, splashing and flailing its legs and hooves. I had never seen a wild animal quite so clumsy. It must have been a humbling experience. The poor thing finally righted itself and bolted over the top of the bank. What a blunder to have to live with!

Several eagles soared across the sky above us, and we noticed one of their nests in a tree on an island. We got a good tongue-lashing for paddling a bit too close. Considering their size and power, we felt lucky the scolding was all we got.

Soon we began to hear the faint thumps and roars of civilization in the distant town. Some of the gray sky was falling on us by that time. The previous day's excessive number of paddling miles had ganged up on our winter-soft bodies. We were both hurting.

Arriving at The Pas feeling as if we had been out for two weeks instead of just two days, we immediately headed for the restaurant and ate a big breakfast. We took our clothes to the laundromat, as if we needed clean clothes to slop around on muddy riverbanks and cook over smokey campfires. But who knew when our clothes would ever see a washing machine again!

We also made an extremely important purchase—a wide-mouth watertight plastic vessel to contain the liquid waste that had so often interrupted our few hours of fitful sleep. We had camped for several years but had never won the late-night Battle of the Bulging Bladder. Both of us usually woke up at the beck and call of each other's discomfort. On cold rainy nights in mosquito-infested camp-sites, Nature first called gently, then became more insistent, and finally screamed, "You fool! Do you want to burst!" Next came the hasty unzipping of the tent opening, the hasty exit, and the hasty rezipping in an effort to keep the mosquitoes on the outside. Then we reversed the procedure and followed it by searching the ceiling of the tent with our penlights for intruders that needed to be destroyed. We took no prisoners. Once in a while we would miss an undercover agent. During the next half hour of interrupted dozing, we would flail our faces and clout our ears whenever the droning seemed close enough to home in on. We probably ran a greater risk of concussion than we did of being bled dry by killer mosquitoes.

A rare picture showing both of us paddling. Taken from the landing at The Pas.

Wayne Hucabuk, a young man who ran the Kinsman Campground at the edge of the river, agreed to take some planned pictures of us paddling in toward the landing at The Pas. They are the only ones we had taken of us in the canoe during the whole trip. Photographers are scarce in the wilderness. He sent us on our way, cheerfully quoting a weather forecast that called for a ninety percent chance of rain. As we passed under the provincial highway bridge, I glanced up at the traffic overhead and wondered how long it might be before we would see that scene again. Ironically, I felt more security in its noise and pollution than I expected from the quiet wilderness we would be traveling through. We were each carrying a mini-tape recorder so that we could keep better records of our daily adventures. I am the one who usually writes the important stuff down in my tiny notebook. I have such a poor memory that I was afraid too many fascinating little details would not be captured for posterity. The tape recorders, however, saved everything we said, whether we had anything to say or not.

Fred wanted me to be sure to record the fact that we had arrived at The Pas at 10:00 A.M. and were leaving at 2:00 P.M. That was almost a transgression of my rights. During the school year, I watch a clock constantly. My job is to solve a variety of learning problems within small time periods allotted to each of the children. The schedule is tight, and usually I am trying to squeeze too much into too little time. Consequently, during the summer months, especially on vacation trips, I often don't wear a watch. We had both declared that we wanted to try to become lost in time. But there was Fred, two days out, still keeping close track of it.

We entered the Summerberry River a few miles out of The Pas. It was a bit smaller than the Saskatchewan, and so were the chances of finding a campsite. Fred finally climbed up a ten-foot riverbank on a game trail and hacked out just enough undergrowth and small saplings to make a space to accommodate the tent. Forget *level* and *smooth!* There was hardly any room around the outside of the tent to set the little cook stove. There wasn't even a place to put the canoe, so he left it in the river and tied each end of it to several bushes. He said if the water came up, the bushes would have to wash away before we would lose the canoe. But we were less particular about our bedroom than we had been, and our weary bodies somehow oozed into places between the bumps for a decent night's rest.

The next morning, Fred said he had heard some snufflings and snortings in the night. I was glad I hadn't heard

Flashing wings and working feet;
Awkward, clumsy, struggling there.

them. I'd been able to talk myself into going to sleep because of a secret ritual I had performed upon our arrival. I
had whipped out my small canister of mace and sprayed a
couple of broad, sweeping strokes in a circle around the
immediate area. It was one of those little acts about which I
often philosophize thusly: "It's like feeding chicken soup
to a dead man—it can't hurt!"

June 21 was cloudy, cold, and windy, probably fifty-
five to sixty degrees Fahrenheit. We followed a pelican pa-
rade on the Summerberry. Several groups of the large
white birds had led the way down the river, but the flock
of eleven was the most memorable. They stayed in group
formation, both swimming and flying. They would float
along until we came within three or four rods of them.

Then one by one, in the order they were lined up, they would splash their big webbed paddles and flop their wide wings until they could get up out of the water. Once airborne, they were transformed into creatures of grace and loveliness. They would glide forever before moving their wings at all. Then each pelican would begin its wing movement in the same order in which it had taken flight. When they started their landing pattern a short distance down the river, they would float on the air just above the water for a long time before meeting the surface with hardly a ripple, as if they were settling into a nest. They would retract their wings and tuck them against their bodies so that they could drift along with the current for awhile.

My tender-heartedness toward animals is forever causing me anguish. Even as a child, I didn't like Lassie movies. I couldn't stand thinking about the pain the poor dog had to go through to save some inept human being. I have a mouse trap that shoves the mice into a storage compartment. Then, humming "Born Free," I drive them to an abandoned house on a country road and turn them loose. It's not just any house; it has bales of nice warm hay in it. However, wild creatures have sometimes humiliated, irritated, and/or frightened the tenderness right out of my heart.

I admit, it is the *idea* of the bear rather than the bear itself that has made me uneasy. I have never been closer than a hundred yards to a wild bear, and that one was leaving hastily with its cub, thank goodness! Gulls have dived at us head-on when we came too close to their eggs. They never made contact, of course. I have accidentally stepped across a sleeping snake, looped and folded into a heap. In an effort to avoid disturbing its sleep, I even suppressed most of my screams.

But BEAVERS—they take the prize! They slap their tales when they are annoyed with campers. They build dams in really nasty spots for canoeists to deal with. They leave a bunch of stumps sticking up in what might have been a beautiful wooded glade. I present these rationales to dispel the notion that cruelty entered into the following trick we played on one of these diabolical animals. Our only objectives were a good laugh and a touch of sweet revenge. One morning while gliding quietly down the river, we saw a large beaver den in the distance. As we drifted nearer, we noticed some ripples near the edge of it and hushed ourselves immediately. Every few seconds, the water would break over a little brown hump, and sometimes a blunt nose would poke out. This miniature construction worker continued his project, oblivious to our approach. I turned slightly toward the back of the canoe in time to see my partner slowly raising his paddle blade high in the air.

Mr. Beaver was still totally involved in his work less than ten feet away when the paddle began its downward rush through the air toward the flat surface of the water. The wide blade leveled off and met the flat water perfectly, producing a resounding WHACK! A large wet blob of fur shot up out of the water gyrating two feet into the air. He seemed to levitate for an instant, his tail thrashing up and down all the while. He finally splashed down, still slapping his tail, and disappeared into his watery home, possibly for the rest of his life. Think of the grudge he must carry toward all canoeists! I, for one, am glad we won't be camping in that area within the next decade.

After hours of paddling without finding a piece of solid ground to stand on, we were willing to land on anything that didn't suck us under completely. For a quick lunch, we settled precariously on a huge deadfall lying along the steep muddy bank. We polished off some peanut butter and jelly sandwiches using our civilized bread, which was fast approaching the antibiotic stage.

At the close of the gourmet feast, Fred made a sudden decision to climb the ten-foot bank for a trip to the woods. Shortly after he disappeared over the crest of the hill, I began to hear more rustling and thrashing than he could ever produce. Loud cracking sounds made by the breaking of limbs at least an inch in diameter were coming from Fred's general vicinity. Of course, because he was making half of the noise, not only was he unable to hear the other half, he was also unable to hear me telling him about it.

"Fred!"

Thrash, thrash. "Ya know, Joyce, this is really a nice wooded area up here—"*Thrash, thrash.*

"Fred! Do you hear—"

Rustle, rustle, crack!

"It'd make an ideal spot for a cabin *(thrash, thrash)* if we could *(mumble, mumble)."*

Rustle, CRACK!

Then came a few seconds of blessed silence with which my next plea coincided.

"Fred! Listen!"

"Huh?'

Praise the Lord! He heard me! "There's something making noises up there," I aimed my stage whisper at the top of the bank.

"Did you say something down there?"

Oh, Brother! Though I was thoroughly disgusted at not being able to make him hear, I still felt obliged to do the honorable thing. I kept trying. I thought I might be saving him from being mauled by a bear or trampled by a moose.

"THERE'S SOMETHING UP THERE!" CR-A-A-CK! "Something *BIG!"* My voice was breaking into high-pitched shrieks. "Let's *GO!"*

"Gosh! Did you hear that! There's something up here!"
He burst from the forest with almost as much haste as
when he had entered it and appeared above me leaping
and sliding down the bank. Immediately taking charge of
the situation, he uttered words repeated down through the
ages by terrified people with any sense at all: "Let's get
outa here!"

We threw the few lunch items in the canoe and began
pushing it off the mud, stern first. When it had nearly
cleared the bank, Fred shoved once more and jumped in. I
almost missed the boat but managed to make a skin-of-the-
seat landing in the bow. We could still hear the crashing
and cracking of sizeable sticks. We swung the canoe
around, and the current carried us away from the scene.
All noises finally subsided: the rustling, the cracking, and
the thundering of my heart. The source of the industrial-
strength commotion that had prompted our hasty departure would forever remain a mystery. Just for an instant,
the Flying Beaver popped into my mind. Could he have
had a giant uncle? *NAH!*

Later that day, we laughed about our state of panic. It
could have been a ticklish escape if Fred's trip to the woods
had been interrupted at a less convenient moment. I personally would have been interested to see if he could have
made his way down the bank and leaped into the canoe
with his pants down around his ankles.

As nearly as we could figure it on the map, we paddled
approximately forty miles and arrived at our campsite in
the usual state, tired and sore. The day was still misty,
gray, windy, and cold. Our little thermometer registered
forty-one degrees by the time we stopped. It was the de-
creasing temperature that aroused in me a faint memory of
an Indian reserve on Moose Lake that Fred had mentioned. I carelessly lapsed into soft, civilized thoughts

about a shelter with a roof on it and maybe running water, and even central heating. In the tent that night, I hinted strongly that we might paddle the extra two miles or so over to the reserve, just to pick up some bread and a couple of other items. My suggestion was met with disdain, but I didn't give up hope completely.

The mentholated balm Fred rubbed on my sore shoulders felt wonderful. I went to sleep thinking of ways to persuade him that all we had to do was paddle up Moose Creek, over to Moose Lake Indian reserve, and we'd be in clover! And hamburgers! And soda pop! And maybe even warm beds!

A lunch break near Moose Lake. I was freezing.

FLIGHT OF A PELICAN

Flopping, rushing toward the air;
Splashing, thrashing, everywhere;
  Flashing wings and working feet;
    Awkward, clumsy, struggling there.

At last, from surface breaking clear;
Legs stretch back straight as a spear;
  Wings fan out and press the air;
    Feathers gently turn to steer.

Airborne, hovering in a glide,
Just above the river wide.
  Bird with bill for hauling freight,
    How easily on air you ride!

Lower now, the white wings drift;
Scarcely any feathers shift.
  Such slow descent when touchdown comes,
    The landing makes but one small rift.

Moose Lake: One Way Or The Other

"**P**addle! hard!" came the command from behind me.

"Are you crazy?" I said. "Those waves are huge!" My reply was lost to the wind because I was afraid even to turn my head to the rear so I could be heard.

"Keep going! We have to get out of the mouth of the creek and onto the lake!" Urgency increased Fred's volume.

We had come 150 miles, give or take a lifetime or two. Up to this point, there hadn't been any real crises, except in my mind. York Factory was still over 450 canoe-miles away, at least.

So there we were, at the end of Moose Creek, facing a rising wall of cold gray water. Dainty waffle-weave ripples ran across it. Strange, the details one notices when one's world is coming to an end! The huge wave had been graciously heaved up for our arrival by the wind blowing across most of the forty-mile length of Moose Lake. This

tidal wave surged toward the canoe almost in slow motion
and then welled up under it, lifting it several feet higher
than my heart and stomach were willing to go.

My Mouth chose that moment in time to make me extremely unpopular with my canoe-mate. In my everyday
life, Mouth often damages my credibility and costs me
hours of lost sleep spent on guilt trips from something it
has said. There, in the middle of that lonely wilderness, it
was leading me into even more disgrace. Blabbing Mouth
set me up to reveal the cowardice I had managed to keep
hidden until then. When the wall of water came up, it
went berserk! It said, "We've got to turn around! We'll
swamp! We can't *do* this!" (It wouldn't let up.) "*I* can't do
this! Let's go back!"

I didn't really have time to focus on the exact vocabu-
lary my husband chose to express his dismay. It came to me
rather suddenly that turning a canoe around in the trough
of an enormous wave was probably not going to offer the
kind of security I so desperately sought at that moment.

Fortune smiled on me, for a change. The canoe turned
quickly and efficiently. The turn was possibly just a miracle, but it might have been expedited by the violent blue
air currents issuing forth vociferously from the stern.

The deed was done, and I was able to reign in Mouth
so that it didn't spew out further incriminating phrases,
such as, "Gee, we probably should have just kept on going
out into the lake. I can see now that the worst part was just
the little area where the current from the creek met the
waves pushing in off the lake."

In spite of Fred's disgust with my attitude and because
of his desperation to continue the trip in some fashion,
though it would be a slightly tarnished venture from that
point on, he remembered a small stream running off of
Moose Creek that would lead to Moose Lake Indian

reserve. We retraced our route a short distance and found the branch of water.

Winding back and forth through the tall grass and watery muskeg in the crooked little stream, I began to reflect on our discussion of the day before about whether or not we would go to the Indian reserve. I was fully aware of how my partner felt about interrupting our wilderness trip with a careless jaunt back into civilization. He had given me a few gentle hints by saying things like, "We don't need to stop at Moose Lake reserve. It will delay us. We won't want to leave. We need to eat the food out of our packs. We're going on!" Because of my loyalty to Fred and a moderate amount of determination to reach our final goal, thoughts of a grocery store, a place to sleep that wouldn't have to be hacked out of a rough, bush-covered riverbank, and maybe even a hot bath, should have made me feel ashamed. Instead, the farther up the little stream we paddled, the better I felt about it. I lapsed into dreams of cold drinks out of a machine, lunch meat sandwiches, and other such decadent pleasures.

I spied a tower, probably a microwave booster of some kind. When I pointed it out, Fred's speech patterns revealed a slight lift in his spirits. He began using words of more than one syllable. Then we began to see buildings, and we both paddled a little harder. By that time, the wind was whipping up a misty rain. The buildings came closer, but the creek began dealing out cute little tricks. Every few feet, a small waterway would veer off of the main stream and snake out through the tall thick grass growing in shallow water. Those little "branches," we call them in Southern Indiana, were all barely wide enough for the canoe and no one more important-looking than the next. The twists and turns were often not even far enough apart to enable us to turn the canoe without backing up and pulling forward two or three times. We tried one branch after another and faced one dead-end after another. I could picture the area as a field laboratory designed for testing the behavior of tired, hungry canoeists working their way through a maze toward food. Scientists with binoculars were probably computing the ratio of wasted energy to forward motion as we awkwardly backed our eighteen-footer out of the weeds, again and again.

After seemingly endless frustration, we emerged from this inundated muskeg jungle into an open expanse of water. Just across it, about a half-mile away, was a crude dock made of logs. Cars were parked on a road, and along the shoreline were some motorboats. Paddling against the wind, we had to command extra strength for our aching limbs to force the canoe across the tiny lake.

A warm feeling of security washed over me as I unfolded my legs for the first time in hours. Fred said, "Hop out and pull us up a little." My grouchy limbs informed me that jumping nimbly out of the canoe and pulling it up on the shore was out of the question, and that I'd be lucky not to embarrass myself by falling flat on whichever part of my anatomy was closest to the ground. In spite of the reluctance of my muscles, I felt pretty good. Those were the delicious moments of newly-acquired stability. I even began to feel that I could someday look back and—no, not *laugh* —but at least come to realize that I had over-reacted to what I thought was an impossible situation, and that the sheer terror which had turned many of my hairs white was based only on my own emotional point of view.

However, even while I was wallowing in that security, somewhere in the dark recesses of my brain, there lurked a tiny splinter of dismay. If I had allowed it to remain embedded there, it would have festered into an ominous thought: *Moose Lake still had to be crossed!* No doubt it would be windy, rainy, and impossible. But at least for the time being, I was okay!

THE DAY WE HIT "THE WALL"

Trying to get onto big Moose Lake
Certainly wasn't a piece of cake!

The current flowed swiftly down little Moose
     Creek;
It met the waves of the lake at their peak.

We paddled right up to a water wall
That made my heart go into a stall.

I chickened out and cried, "Oh, *NO!*
Across that wave, we just can't go!"

"We've got to turn the canoe around;
My day will be ruined if I am drowned!"

So back we went, retracing our way.
My mate was not happy with wifey that day!

Three times as far, four times as long,
Our move toward the goal was not very strong.

A maze of dead-ends in a channel too small;
Corners were blind, the grass was too tall.

Nose in, back out; use the paddle to pry
Away from the muskeg to current nearby.

Exhausted, discouraged, we worked our way
     through
To spaces wide open, and then the wind blew

Right in our faces and made it all tougher!
No grass or high banks to serve as a buffer.

Bodies were tired and spirits were down,
It took us forever to reach the small town.

But there, at last, was a dock and a road,
Cars and buildings and grass that was mowed!

Sore and disheartened, we stepped on dry land.
I was relieved to be able to stand.

It wasn't the place Fred had wanted to be.
He only went there because of *me*.

If I'd known the wind would hold us four days,
I wouldn't have wished to be at that place.

But we made new friends and learned some
    background
Of the people we met and the country around.

It turned out okay. We ate and we rested.
I felt the time there had been well invested.

Breaking
The Spell

Fred had been right, again.
Being stuck in a small village with a nice room to sleep in, a kitchen to cook in, a piano to play, TV and VCR movies to watch, and even dogs to pet could easily dissuade a person from finishing a wilderness canoe trip in a summerless country.

I have a few favorite recipes at home that I use every year or so when the "happy homemaker" awakens in me like a cobra rising out of sleep. But except for those times when my soul has been possessed by that evil influence, I would just as soon eat out. The lodge where we stayed had been fashioned from a large house and was used to accommodate hunting and fishing groups. An enormous kitchen was equipped with a huge gas range, gigantic iron cooking vessels, two large galvanized sinks, two refrigerators, and five heavy duty appetites. Two of the appetites belonged to Greg and Peter McAfee, the sons of the owner of the lodge and the grandsons of Tom Lamb, famous in that area for being the former owner of the first sizeable airline and for promoting the growth and maintenance of that portion of the North Country. The other three appetites belonged to Otis and Steve, two traveling construction workers stationed there to build a nursing center, and "Gus" Gustafason, an employee and long-time friend of the McAfee family.

The house was deserted most of the time during the day because everyone went outside or somewhere else to work. Perhaps I was left alone in the immense kitchen to test some kind of theory, like the one about a tree falling in the forest. If no one is near enough to hear it, is sound produced? If a woman is left in a kitchen in the middle of a wilderness, and no one is nearby to put pressure on her, will food be prepared?

I wasn't really expected to cook for everyone, but I was looked at with a kind of hunger that I couldn't, by any stretch of my imagination, interpret as lust for my body. So I did cook—not fancy stuff, of course. It was a meager assortment of plain and simple fare, but it went over big. In fact, it was reported to me by a friend nearly a year later that she had become acquainted with the two traveling construction workers and that they had remembered meeting us. They even mentioned how good my beef stew had tasted!

Three dogs made up the pet set. The most interesting one was Big Mike, a gentle black Labrador Retriever who carried around empty plastic bottles that had been dropped in the yard and rocks he "retrieved" from the lake. Later in the trip, we met Big Mike's brother Duke.

The day after we arrived was a bright calm Sunday complete with church bells ringing. It had already been designated the night before as our day of rest. The next four mornings, the weather was a nasty combination of wind and rain. At dawn, we would check out the lake from the upstairs bathroom window, grumble a bit, and go back to bed. Finally, Fred could bear it no longer. "We're going tomorrow morning," he said, on the fourth evening. His statement had a ring of finality about it that squelched my response. I wanted to say, "But shouldn't we wait and see about the weather?" What came out was a tiny, "Okay."

During our stay at the lodge and throughout the remainder of the trip, Fred felt guilty about not living every minute of it in the rough: that is, not braving the elements and cooking over our little stove or a campfire every single day and night. We had seen a newspaper cartoon featuring a group of hard-core marathon runners—the kind that look as if they have been on a thirty-day hunger strike. Their running suits drooped on their skinny bodies, and their hollow eyes looked out of gaunt faces. Having run in a few short races ourselves, we could appreciate the likeness. In the cartoon, an official with a bullhorn was announcing the layout of the course. It was to be run through the desert for something like fifty miles, with no drinking water provided. One of the runners complained that it would be too easy. He said, "Why don't we do it without shoes! Oh, please, let us do it without shoes!"

So the official gave in and said, "Oh, all right. You can do it without shoes." The emaciated runners all looked pleased with that arrangement.

Fred wanted to do our whole trip without shoes. But having read about how well organized the tripmen were, I thought they surely must have tried to make things as comfortable for themselves as possible under the circumstances. After Samuel Hearne and the boys had made one or two trips to Cumberland House, they surely were smart enough to build some semi-permanent shelters along the way. A few years later, several fur posts were built on the route. So even those early travelers had a chance to sleep under-roof once in awhile. After all, if the gentlemen at

York Factory dined in full-dress uniforms twice a week as guest of the Governor of the Day, didn't we have the right to sleep in a bed for a few nights without blowing our image as modern-day voyageurs?

We headed out, keeping a short distance from the shoreline. We crossed the moderately choppy waves and maneuvered past the turbulent waters at the mouth of Moose Creek, where I had turned chicken and squawked at the wall of water. It wasn't smooth, but it looked a heck of a lot better than it had from the other side five days before. Then we crossed a sizeable hunk of open water to gain the lee of the big island, the other side of which would put us in good position to go down the length of South Moose Lake. We made good work of it and then stopped for a pleasant lunch on a rock beach. Some Cree fishermen in a motorboat stopped by and chatted for a few minutes.

We continued around the big island until we were no longer in the shelter of it. The waves blowing across each other diagonally from behind two different islands began trying to toss us in several different directions at once. The choppy water was further agitated by waves rebounding from the shoreline. The *Hoosier Transit* was doing weird things in all of that nasty heaving stuff, but it stuck on the water like glue, never lofting any part of itself. The slender little bow was darting left and right spasmodically. I was just as spasmodic in trying to figure out on which side of the canoe to paddle in order to keep us moving forward. My stern paddler was responsible for any hint of efficiency that was strong enough to override my thrashing and blundering in the bow. If he hadn't been such a "stern" paddler, we might still be out there, in one form or another, for it was solely at his urging that I kept going as long as I did. I was exhausted.

We stopped for a snack on a sunny rock beach before resuming the battle with wind and wave. We were beginning to notice that the name on our canoe was more appropriate than we had ever thought it would be. The original *Hoosier Transit* was a small trucking company owned by Fred's father in the early 30's. It was one of the first freight lines to run between Louisville, Kentucky, and small towns in Indiana like Paoli, Bedford, and Jasper. Our *Hoosier Transit* was hauling its paddlers and its 237 pounds of freight across the North Country with more security and stability than we had thought possible.

HOOSIER TRANSIT

For our wilderness canoe,
     We chose a special name.
We called it *Hoosier Transit*,
     Remembering family fame.

Stone and Williams Transfer
     In the "20's" was begun.
The truckline was the first
     That Hoosier route to run.

Louisville, Bedford, Jasper;
     Trucks rolled from dawn to dawn.
Fred's father ran the firm;
     Alone he carried on.

The name was *Hoosier Transit*;
     It grew to be first rate.
Deep snow and icy weather
     Would never halt the freight.

A perfect choice, that name.
     It represented true
How well we hauled our freight
     In spite of winds that blew.

The title made us proud;
     It saw us safely through.
Fred's father would have smiled
     At the name on our canoe.

Three-Day Island

By the time we finally reached a small island in eternal Moose Lake, I had only an ounce and a half of strength left, the exact amount that was needed for building a fire and starting supper. Fred carried the canoe up over a row of rocks piled three feet high along the edge of the island. The levy of rocks had been rolled up by high waves during storms. During the next several days, we would realize that this ridge was a primitive warning which translated into, "Caution: This island is a wind trap. It may be hazardous to your mental health."

The food packs didn't resist my invasion except for the usual pouting buckle or stubborn flap, but each motion sapped an enormous amount of strength from my bone-weary body. I managed to get something extremely short of a gourmet feast together using the pile of rocks as a fire-place. After staring for awhile at the gray sky and choppy waters, we decided to hang it up for the night before the North Country Blood Bank sent out its flying collection agency. The wind hissed through the trees above the tent, but I drifted off to sleep, confident that the next day would bring brighter prospects for paddling.

Wrong! Gray, wet, and windy! I looked through the trees from behind the rocky waterfront property. Actually, we had a nicely protected area for the tent, "down in" the island. It was less blustery in the dark interior, but even in that secluded area, a shelter of stones had to be built up around the tiny campfire to keep it from being whipped about and extinguished by the gusty wind. Everything was so damp that we were certainly in no danger of setting fire to the forest or, for that matter, any of the wood we were trying to burn in our tiny fireplace. So we crawled back in the tent. Maybe noon would bring a little calming or clearing.

Noon: Rain. Cooked a little meal. Slept some more. Surely, tomorrow!

Nope. Drizzle. Gray sky. White caps. A soggy tour of the island revealed several large patches of animal sign. There was quite a bit of speculation in my mind as to the shape and size of the animal who was responsible for it. To quiet my misgivings, Fred tried to convince me it was "moose." But I suspected that he just didn't want to admit that it was "bear" because he didn't want to spend the rest of the day on the island with a nervous bow paddler nursing a shotgun. He even reassured me that the bear den we came across was an old one from the previous winter, long-since vacated.

Then something strange and unpleasant began happening to me. I gradually became more depressed than I had ever been in my life. That kind of feeling was unnatural to me, but for some reason, I couldn't overcome it. Even before we left home, I had anticipated being stuck in the tent with nothing to do during bouts of bad weather. For just such occasions, I had recorded a special mini tape containing excerpts from my favorite radio show, "Prairie Home Companion," and some selections from a Louisville Symphony Orchestra concert. But there on that dismal island, I was so afraid I might become hysterically homesick that I thought I couldn't bear to hear the voices and sounds of things I loved.

Fred would look into the face of a zombie and say, "Honey, do you think maybe you'd want to cook us a little dinner?" I could tell he was puzzled, too. He asked me several times if I was all right. I think he was getting a little worried that I might sink so low that neither of us could deal with it. For the first time in my life, I had a small glimpse of what a paralyzing effect deep depression can have, not only on the mind, but also on the body. My arms and legs were like lead weights. I had to force myself to move from one place to another, to open a bag, to pick up firewood. I fought against sitting motionless and staring at the gray mist across the lake until I was shivering in the cold damp air. A scene which I had thought beautiful on so many other occasions was now eating away at my morale. I tried hard to keep my thoughts positive and my mind busy with small plans, but even working at improving my mental outlook was an overwhelming task.

Day number three. Gray, ugly. Tent-bound. No hope. They'll find our bones here. Food running low. Counted the packages again. Same number. Only enough for thirty-seven more days. How many days would we live after it ran out?

Tent fever amplifies small sounds and magnifies tiny annoyances that don't even register in a person's mind after he has just finished a satisfying day of paddling and is tired enough to sleep. The little string that holds the tent flap back was untied. For hours, it flapped tediously in the wind. I stared at the mosquitoes we had mashed on the ceiling of the tent two weeks before. I'd logged every sound, every movement, the weather, the scenery. I was down to scrawling out depressing rhymes with jumbled metaphors. I forced a nap on my restless brain. I played with the first-aid kit. Read up on CPR. Napped again. Finally got the fire going in the drizzle. Cooked some beans. That took up about two hours. Fascinating. Talked Fred into playing blackjack with a set of survival cards. The game was even less absorbing than reading the material printed on them, instructions for reviving a drowning victim, first-aid procedures to relieve frostbite, etc. I didn't push for that kind of excitement again. If we were going to die, I'd rather be mauled by a bear than to be found with a queen and an ace in my hand and a yawn on my face.

The next morning we would go. Early, to beat the wind. Up at dawn. And . . . *away!* Clear skies, smooth water. The spell was broken. I was alive again!

We finished off the first hitch of the forty-mile lake and arrived at the narrows by mid-morning. Nothing boring about a canoe trip!

THE JAILER

*Written during a "blow" on a little island
June 28, 1985*

The cold wind shows no mercy;
    It blows through leaf and limb.
It pushes surface water
    Over shores at its own whim.

The treetops rage against it;
    The waves roll back for more;
White gulls hang in mid-air,
    Above the water's roar.

The wind's strong teeth are bared,
    And with a breathy growl
It shatters rain to mist,
    And drives on with a howl.

Wind and *Fire* and *Water*
    And *Earth* are everything.
Wind is a part of life,
    It makes the winter sing;

Its breeze cools summer brows;
    In spring it melts the snow;
But the jailer that tends this isle
    Is the cruelest wind I know.

Its fury has been raging;
    Pounding, tearing the land.
Smashing the water on rocks;
    Hoping to wear them to sand.

Incessant roar in the treetops
    Blocks out our favorite sounds.
One brave bird trills brightly;
    Warmth from its descant resounds.

The wind sings his stormy song,
    Louder than any worth mention;
Lonely, demanding, insistent
    On our undivided attention.

Its timbre wearies our bodies;
    We're cold, and tired of its role
That dominates our being,
    Suppresses the life in our souls.

But when the wind has ceased
    His bombastic symphony,
The Jailer's bonds we'll escape;
    From prison at last we'll be free!

Little House On The Lake

When we were at the lodge, we had heard Peter McAfee mention that there was some kind of cabin at the narrows of Moose Lake. Through the mist on that Sunday morning, we saw a red two-story house surrounded by a lawn, flower beds, and vegetable garden. A black retriever was coming to the dock to greet us. Doris and "Doc" Meriweather came out and invited us into their home. They had just finished breakfast, but there was some pancake batter left, and they asked if we would like a pancake or two. While Fred was drawing a breath to say that he didn't want them to go to any trouble, I inserted a resounding, "Yes!"

The retriever's name was Duke. He was a brother to Big Mike, who lived at McAfee's lodge. Doc had helped train both dogs to retrieve ducks when they were young. He said the dogs would go after the ducks that had been downed, and each dog would put his ducks in his own pile. Then when Duke was busy, Big Mike would sneak a duck or two from Duke's pile and add it to his own. Duke would notice it and take the ducks back to his pile. When the McAfee boys were children, they would throw rocks into the lake, and the dogs would go after them. The boys are grown now, but the dogs often still go into the water and pick up rocks to carry.

The Meriweathers had finished building their house in about 1954 and had stayed in it for several weeks each summer and sometimes in the fall and spring. Among other things, the house boasted a comfortable sitting area, two bedrooms, a big iron cookstove, and an upright piano. This last item had been transported on a small barge up the Saskatchewan River from The Pas and then up Moose Creek and around Moose Lake, the route we had just traveled. The piano had been dismantled as much as possible and then reassembled. A tuner came out to the place by motor boat and dried out the wet pads for a long time with a hair dryer before he could put it back in working order.

The house also had an indoor bathroom. That didn't seem unnatural except that the sewer system was built up on logs and blocks sloping down from the second story of the house and into a disposal unit. Dirt that had been hauled in by barge was heaped over the drainage "box." Asparagus plants were growing in it. There were several other garden areas, all of which had to be fenced in to keep wild animals from devouring everything.

Sitting in a chair at a table was nice. I don't mind sitting on the ground or a log or a flat rock, but I was glad to have a break from bending over a pot of boiling water or trying to hang on to a hot pan handle or doing CPR on a dying fire with smoke-tears running down my face.

When we began to tear ourselves loose from this little Brigadoon, our hostess saw Fred looking lovingly at the collection of books on their shelves. She asked if we'd like to borrow a couple to take with us. I had said earlier that I wished I had brought something to read during times like the Three-Day Island stint we had just completed. We took a couple of paperbacks, and promised to return them, not guaranteeing that they would be in perfect condition. We wrapped them tightly in plastic "locking" bags. For the rest of the trip, whenever we finished reading them for the evening, we rewrapped them carefully and put them deep in our packs. The books survived the canoe trip in excellent condition, and we mailed them back to the Meriweathers when we returned home. About a year and a half later, we learned that the package in which we had mailed them had been mangled. We weren't sure if the books themselves made it from Indiana to the Meriweathers' regular home in South Dakota.

We had tried to find out at Moose Lake where the portage into the Minago River started and what condition it was in. No one there knew much about it. The Meriweathers gave us a few pointers, but they said they just hadn't traveled that direction in a long time.

So off we went, hoping the dark cloud chipping away at the sun wouldn't rain on us. But it did. We stopped for lunch on the bank of the north arm of Moose Lake. The water was crystal green from the limestone. Great piles of rock had been heaped up by the waves during storms, much like the natural levy we had camped behind on Three-day Island. We heated up the left-over beans on two of the rocks propped up on either side of a tiny fire I had managed to kindle in spite of the drizzle.

By early evening, we had finished paddling the length of Moose Lake. We explored the end of it and, in preparation for the next day, located Pine Creek where we would paddle towards the portage area. Then we made camp on a rocky little point which belonged to a beaver. During the course of our stay, the irate landowner made several obscene beavertail comments. The loud *ker-plunking* just offshore was an effective communiqué, especially at 1:00 A.M.

The campsite wasn't half bad, though by this time our specs for the tolerable campsite had been downgraded a couple of notches. If the place was big enough to accommodate the floor of the tent and was not below the water level of the lake, we grabbed it. The tent site on this one had to be hacked out and whipped down among a bunch of bushes and weeds. There were wild rose bushes all around, which was reason enough not to emerge from the tent at night, for any reason. Fred picked a rose and gave it to me. I stuck it in my stocking cap. It set off the khaki shirt and muddy white pants beautifully and was just the right shade of pink to bring out the scarlet tones of my sunburned nose. I was the best-dressed woman canoeist on the north arm of Moose Lake.

The main course of our supper was canned elk meat that Doris had sent with us. For the rest of the trip, we had to carry the glass jar it had been packed in. (We have never allowed ourselves to litter any area where we have camped.) But the treat was worth it. The meat was sweet and smooth.

We were filled with anticipation of paddling down the Minago River. Of course, there was the small matter of locating and crossing the portage, but on the map it looked as if the distance between bodies of water couldn't be more than a mile and a half. No sweat. We finally turned in and slept—between *ker-plunks*.

DISGRACEFUL BEHAVIOR

"You BEAST!" I shouted.
　　He gestured obscenely,
Flashing his backside
　　In manner unseemly!

From sleep he had jarred me
　　With noises quite rude.
Disgusted, I was,
　　At behavior so crude!

Hiding and waiting
　　To crush my ego!
And thinking up tricks;
　　He was laughing, I know!

"Just leave me alone!
　　Get out of my sight!
Go! Let me sleep
　　The rest of this night!

I don't need you here.
　　You're just too much trouble!
I'm happy without you.
　　Does that burst your bubble?

You're bold and obnoxious,
　　A show-off, a ham!
Y'know, Mr. Beaver,
　　You ain't worth a *dam!*"

Minago Portage

The curves in the narrow little stream were so sharp that sometimes we took shortcuts through patches of the partially submerged clumps of grass, pushing and prying until we were floating free again. Pine Creek was probably less than a mile and a quarter long, but it was a long mile and a quarter! We ate a bite of lunch in the canoe on the water. No choice about that. There was no place to step out on dry or even solid ground. After working our way around the many curves and through the muck, even the too-familiar peanut butter and pancake lunch tasted pretty good. The novelty of passing it bow to stern on a paddle blade took away some of the sameness of that particular meal.

Pine Creek emptied into Pine Lake, scarcely bigger than an Indiana farm pond. We crossed it and looked for a good landing spot. After a brief search, we canceled the "good" in that phrase and tried to pick the least of all evils which proved to be a memorable hundred-yard walk, hip-deep in watery gook. That combination of earth, grass roots, and water is known as *muskeg*. We were elated when we could once again put both feet on solid ground at the same time.

We parked our gear temporarily so that we could scout around for a hint of a portage trail.

"Gee, I hope someone doesn't steal all our stuff!" I quipped.

The edge of my partner's humor had evidently been honed down a bit farther than mine. He shot a glance at me that communicated clearly how immature I was. It was no time to laugh!

During the two weeks we had been out, I had heard Fred questioning several different people about the portage from Pine Lake to the headwaters of the Minago River. Most of them would squint their eyes and wrinkle their brows and say something like, "Hm-m-m. A portage to the Minago River. I remember there used to be one . . . let me see . . . where *was* that, now? It's been *years*—"

We studied the topographical map again and came up with the same estimate—a mile and a half across land, as the crow flies. I figured the river ought not to be too hard to find. Fred didn't seem bothered so much about being able to cover the distance as he was about finding a suitable passage from lake to river. What I didn't realize was that not very many other people even cared about where the river began, and it soon became obvious that they cared even less about getting to it from Pine Lake. There was not one clue—not a blade of grass trampled down, not a twig broken—no sign of a trail through that jungle.

After a fruitless hour of walking through soupy mud and clumps of willows and fir saplings, we decided we'd better go back and start packing the gear toward the general direction of the Minago River. If we had left the stuff too far behind with only the compass to guide us back, we might have missed it by going too far to one side or the other. The trees were so thick that we could have walked within a few yards of the bags and not even seen them. Though darkness was several hours away, we knew we'd probably need most of that time to make our way through the jagged branches to some kind of solid ground. It was frustrating and tiring to have our feet either squishing down into mud as soft as fresh cement or sliding off the clumps of grass into icy water. The permafrost must have still been frozen just below the surface.

Fred went on ahead a short distance leaving his menacing, 120-pound hulk of a woman behind to guard the gear bags. Of course, none of us "old bags" was in serious danger from alien influences. I did become useful as a signaling device which enabled Bwana to get a fix on where the gear and I were located. We performed this cooperative process in several hitches. Carrying at least one pack, he would walk ahead and leave it in a place he thought he could find again. On the way back, he would begin calling out to me. As soon as I could hear his voice, I would answer, and he would zero in on my location. Then we would both load up and burrow our way slowly to where he had left his pack. We were like an inch worm, the front stretching ahead and the rear dragging itself up to meet it. Because the initial trail-crashing was concentrated around making a route wide enough to accommodate the canoe, it was usually the last item to go.

The process involved a good deal of tolerance on my part for waiting indefinite periods of time for indefinite news about what lay ahead. The arrangement also called for nerves capable of standing up to strange creaking noises, which usually turned out to be limbs of trees rubbing together as they moved in the breeze—a breeze, incidentally, which couldn't penetrate the thick growth of saplings to stir the hot humid air down where the wildlife and I were making things interesting for one another.

During these periods of waiting three hours for fifteen minutes to pass, I was extremely uneasy. In spite of the fact that I had a faithful companion in the form of a moose fly (they are called moose flies in the North Country because they are the size of a moose), I felt quite alone. Then the bushes would rustle nearby, and I'd wish very much that I felt more alone. I exhumed my tin flute from my hip belt and began tweedling out a few clumsy tunes which I counted on to drive away anything that wasn't deaf. The piping also became another homing device for Fred.

When I was alone, I felt myself shrinking in size and courage. I wanted to make myself seem bigger and more threatening, so I'd pick up a paddle and thump it on the ground or knock it against a tree, gently, of course, so as not to break it. I certainly didn't want to be up *that* creek without one! I hoped the hollow "bonk" would be an intimidating sound to all large animals with antlers, large teeth, hooves, or claws, who were closing in on me from all sides by that time. I kept hoping I could make myself believe Fred's favorite slogan by repeating it over and over: "They're more afraid of me than I am of them. They're more afraid of me. . . . They're more. . . ." But I kept slipping into, "There's no place like home. There's no place like. . . ." I knew I was losing it when my heels began clicking together.

Then I would hear a real crashing of brush and sticks getting louder and closer. I knew it had to be something big! Even after it turned out to be Fred several times, I would still brace myself until I heard his voice or caught sight of the beloved brown felt hat.

My partner and guide finally came to the conclusion that he wasn't going to find a portage trail to the Minago River that day. He thought we'd better start looking for a square of ground solid enough for our tent. I couldn't imagine finding such a phenomenon in the midst of all that watery gush we'd been walking, stumbling, and slogging though most of the afternoon. But it would soon be the Hour of the Mosquito, and we needed to be inside the tent in order to appreciate their evening performance. They would appear in the proscenium of the tent opening, sniffing and poking their snorkels through the netting. Then they would drone their most popular number, "If I said you had a beautiful body, would you hold it against me?"

Fred located a hunk of land. It looked great. It had a few tiny flaws, as real estate property goes, the main one being that it lay at the base of a hill and was on an incline of about thirty degrees. But what the heck! We were going to be there only a few hours and then move right on to the Minago River in the morning.

We spent a relatively peaceful night on that spot, or at least in close proximity to it. We kept sliding downhill. I had a nightmare about slipping into the muskeg. Around 1:00 A.M., I sat up and grabbed Fred. I said, "Hold on! This end is going in!" He convinced me otherwise, and I slept better after that.

Much to my surprise, morning arrived and I wasn't even dead! It was a beautiful day. No rain. Even bright sunshine to keep the mosquitoes subdued. Maybe I was dead! But then we started the search again, and I knew it was all real. We climbed up the hill. Nothing. Not a sign or a hint of a trail at all. We came down and looked further. No water flowing anywhere.

Finally, we came to a willowy swamp. We thought at first it might be something. After wading knee-deep for a quarter of a mile, we gave it up. Once more we moved the gear in the direction of the Minago. We found a dandy campsite that time. Cold drinking water not far away. A large open space on top of a hill with a breeze sweeping across it. Lots of tall trees nearby. Good sleeping. The breeze soughed through the pine trees all night. We heard a loon over in Pine Lake. It was a little depressing to hear how close it sounded after we had been walking for a day and a half trying to get away from that lake. But we would definitely find the way tomorrow! At least by that time, we knew several directions *not* to go.

Day broke. Cloudy skies threatened rain. We had decided that it was pretty risky to get too far away from camp without anything more than a compass to get us back. Even on the shortest of portages, in that thick spruce woods, it was difficult to retrace an unmarked passage when we needed to make more than one trip to transport all of the gear. I had a hard time even following Fred as he battled his way through the bush. Jagged spruce branches would snap together behind him, and he would suddenly be out of my sight.

I had begun to notice many long miles before, that my own legs were quite different from the legs which were always either gradually leaving me behind or quickly overtaking me on those rare occasions when I was lucky enough to get a head start. Often, I'd be returning from my first trip across the portage, and the other legs, on their second trip across, would meet me halfway. One major difference had to do with their length. Those other legs could easily clear large deadfalls in a single step. I had to sidle up to the fallen tree and hope for a smooth sitting area, as opposed to a trunk full of sharp snags. I'd fling one leg over after the other and slide off the other side. The other legs could dance lightly from one slippery rock to another in a shallow stream. The same rocks would taunt me and seem to move farther apart as I approached them. "Go ahead, leap!" I'd say to myself. Then I'd realize that my legs disagreed with me on the definition of the word *leap*. Or, I'd begin stepping across a low branch with leg number one. I always had the highest hopes that leg number two would execute the maneuver equally well. My hopes, along with my shins, elbows, and nose, were often dashed onto whatever surface was the roughest and most unyielding.

Since we move at such vastly different rates, speed became quite a controversial issue. We found it impossible to travel at the same pace, and we frequently became geographically separated. There were even a few times when I decided I could do without my partner's companionship. However, the fact that the canoe was too heavy for me to carry handily by myself made him a necessary item. I also had to admit that things outside the tent that went "bump in the night" (not to mention rustle, crunch, and grunt) were not nearly so loud simply because he was there. I definitely wanted any separation to be extremely temporary, geographical or otherwise.

Because of the risk of misplacing our gear and possibly each other, we decided that we would need some markers for the trail. They would have to be obvious markers, not a broken branch or a heelprint in the dirt every quarter of a mile like the ones the Native Americans followed in the old Western movies.

For once, we actually needed something I had brought for emergencies. I pulled out the fluorescent orange, chartreuse, and shocking pink fabric that I had originally bought for making stuff sacks. The day I brought it home from the fabric store, Fred had chanted one of his favorite phrases that systematically wove itself in and out of our preparations: "That'll never work." His objection was that the sacks wouldn't be waterproof. So I had brought along the pieces to use for signaling airplanes "just in case. . . ."

Those swatches, torn in strips and tied to tree branches would be perfect markers. Hansel-and-Gretel style, we left them behind us so that we could find our way "back home."

A strange quirk of fate brought out one more difference between Fred and me. The fluorescent orange strips worked well for both of us, but even though I started tearing the strips skinnier and skinnier, I finally ran out of that color. From the two remaining swatches, I selected the shocking pink, which I thought would contrast most with the tree leaves. That particular hue would have screamed, *"Here I am!"* to anyone except Fred, whose light-sensitive lenses in his glasses distorted certain bizarre shades of red and green. As we tried to retrace our trail by following the markers, he couldn't see the pink strips unless he was right on top of them, or until I pointed them out to him. And if I tried to go in front, I was like a Bench-leg Beagle leading a Greyhound. It was too hard on both of us. I would nearly die trying to go faster than I could, and he would nearly die trying not to run over me. So, we switched to the chartreuse. But to me, those strips blended perfectly with the bright green leaves on the young trees. I just couldn't see them. Lo and behold! Fred could!

At the end of the third day, we still hadn't located a trail. We began to toy with the idea of building a more permanent residence, something that would keep out the winter cold and snow when it arrived in just two short months. We were being facetious, but we both realized that there would be times in our future when we would wish ourselves back on that mossy knoll in the woods with no more obligations than to plod around all day looking for a river.

The next morning we got up and resumed our work. We'd been beating the bushes for about an hour when the loon flew over again. We exchanged a few pleasantries about loons. Then one of us wondered out loud where it was going. Fred checked his compass and found that it was flying in a northeasterly direction. An idea began to blossom. Loons don't fly around looking for bugs in the woods or road-killed rabbits. They fly from one body of water to another. The only other sizeable body of water on the map was Moon Lake. The loon must be making regular flights between Pine Lake and Moon Lake. The map showed the Minago River flowing into Moon Lake. Therefore, we reasoned, if we could find Moon Lake, we would find the Minago. Hope reborn, we started walking in that direction.

Then I saw a strange-looking contour of land ahead. It was white. Crushed stone. It was a—*road*? I'd been in the bush too long. It would go away. A big white gravel road?

Fred toting the canoe down the road
toward the Minago River

Out here? .... Loggers! They could tell us where that stupid river began! And well they might have, except they were nowhere to be found.

By this time in the trip, we were having to count back to figure out what day of the week it was. Saturday, Monday, and Wednesday were no different from each other. Once in awhile, it would occur to me that it was Sunday, and I'd think of women in light summer dresses and men in shirt sleeves sitting in the Sellersburg United Methodist Church singing hymns. But we usually just kept on truckin' and didn't concentrate on thoughts of home very much. On one of those days, I once again stooped to writing rhymes:

JULY 4

The same wind that held us back
Cooled our brows today.
We walked the long road in the sun,
Trying to find our way.

And so forth. There were three more stanzas of heartfelt comments on why the wind was "better" because it kept our sweat-soaked shirts from getting "wetter."

We lost our perspective on the days of the week, but we were all too much aware of how many days we had spent on the lifelong Minago portage. Day number four ended. My feet were glad of it, having been terribly blistered from walking several miles on the hot gravel road, first in one direction and then back the other way. Long Legs walked twice as far as Wimpy Wife. She simply waited to die and let her skeleton be picked clean by the ravens. The black scavengers had been rasping and croaking for hours, planning their strategy for moving in after it was all over.

In our travels up and down the road, we came to several log yards where heavy equipment was stored. But people? Forget it! It was as if all of the loggers had been snarfed up by a space ship. And what really messed up our minds was the fact that the road was not shown on the map. For a long time, we assumed the Minago was somewhere on the side of the road from which we had originally approached it, since the map showed no road at all but plainly showed the Minago. We finally came to the conclusion that the road had been built after the map had been made. That revelation helped a little but not much. Should we cross the road and start looking? Should we follow the road until it crossed a river? Which direction should we go if we followed it?

We did the one thing we knew we could do and not go wrong. We camped beside the road. We would have put the tent smack in the middle of the road, but if even one lone person in a pickup truck wandered out that way, he would undoubtedly come barreling down the road and run over both of us in our sleep before either of us had a chance to ask directions to the Minago River. We even stripped off our sweat-soaked clothes and bathed in the lukewarm rainwater standing in the big ditch beside the road. I thought if a work crew happened to be nearby, they would not be able to resist coming closer to gaze wantonly upon my nude form. No one came near. I like to assume there *was* no work crew nearby.

We slept undisturbed—no traffic! But we did awaken refreshed to day number five. We were ready to try, try again. We just *knew* we would find it. Were we discouraged? *Yes!*

By that time, we had started searching on the other

side of the road and had finally entered the woods in the most promising area, which was like taking a choice seat in a briar patch. The marker ribbons that had been salvaged from previous trails were badly raveled and knotted. The nylon threads would wrap around the rough pine limbs until they were impossible to separate from the bark and needles. I regret that some of those trees still have strands of ugly shocking colors left in them as a reminder that the Stones passed that way. We tried to make no permanent dents in the wilderness. Occasionally we left some fire-blackened stones and sticks, but then, so did the Indians over three hundred years ago. At least neither they nor we left *plastic* stuff lying around. It doesn't speak well of our current generations that two centuries from now archaeologists will know what brands of shampoo and deodorant our culture used.

We battered our way through the woods following an animal trail used most recently by a moose with huge hooves and a rather disgusting lack of toilet training. The animal that had started the path hadn't been particular about where he planted his feet. He kept on a fairly straight path that honored no obstacles. His trail went through scratchy tree branches, down the center of a shallow stream for about an eighth of a mile, across a bog of muskeg, and among more trees. But then things actually began to look a little less discouraging. The tree tops up ahead were thinning a bit, and as we continued, a genuine opening began to widen out in front of us. My heart did a flip. Could it be a body of . . . ? *No!* A closer look into the opening revealed a large log yard, full of large logs.

We started out across the soggy ground littered with huge obstacles to short legs. At least we were blessed with a breeze to keep the mosquitoes away, but the logs scattered in every direction tried our mettle. Finding a reason-

Fred, satisfied after finding the Minago.

able way around and between these fallen derelicts was worse than Christmas shopping at K-Mart. Jumping from one to the other was catastrophic for me. But repeatedly dragging unwilling legs up and over proved to be an extraordinary endurance test.

While we were skirting the yard looking for a reasonable passage across it, Fred discovered an opening into the woods, a kind of vague overgrown roadway. He followed it and I followed him at my usual lagging pace. He outdistanced me quickly, but suddenly I heard him up ahead yelling something unintelligible. I caught up with him and couldn't believe what I saw. A tiny lake! He said he didn't know if it was just a pond or if it might lead into the Minago River. He told me to wait there while he walked around the rim to see if there was a stream running out of it somewhere. He started off, crashing through the willows. Then he shouted at me to look. I saw him emerge into a cleared area directly across the pond. He said he was standing on a beaver dam and on the other side was a stream big enough to float a canoe. It had to be an entrance to the Minago! We confirmed our victory and shouted congratulations across the lake:

"This is it! We did it!"

"Are you *sure?*"

"It's *gotta* be!"

"You found it! You're my hero!"

We dipped our water bottles in the clear lake and drank a toast to Progress. Back in business! Never mind that we would have to carry all the gear across the log yard, balancing on logs, sinking into muck. Buffeted by the wind, My Hero would leap from one log to the next with the canoe on his back. But who cared about what had to be done next! We were gonna *move!*

SEARCHING!

"The trail's not marked on any chart,"
"But," said Fred, "deep in my heart,
I know we'll find it once we start
    Searching for the Minago."

We crossed Pine Lake and looked around,
But portage trail could not be found,
Nor *any* patch of solid ground,
    Leading to the Minago.

We dragged our gear through muskeg deep;
The muck around our legs would seep,
But still we knew we had to keep
    On searching for the Minago.

We slogged and hacked our way along;
Each way we'd try would turn out wrong!
We combed the woods for three days long,
    Searching for the Minago.

Then at last, a road we spied!
Were we in Heaven? Had we died?
What fun to walk on road so wide!
    Searching for the Minago.

That road turned out to be a "bummer."
We could have walked on it all summer!
Four days were gone. We felt much dumber,
    Searching for the Minago.

That night the loon sang as it flew
To lake we thought we surely knew.
We mocked his navigation true,
    And searched for the Minago.

Our instincts on the loon proved sound;
In that direction we were bound;
Then Fred sang out, "It's *here!* We've found
The start of the Minago."

Back
On the
Water

At last, we were riding in the canoe again instead of walking under it. All went well, until we arrived at the real Minago River about five miles later. I thought it should have been a bit more impressive than the shallow little stream rippling over a bed of shale ten feet wide. We started down it, good-naturedly ducking a few overhead branches, generously giving the river a chance to deepen and widen itself to make canoe travel more expeditious. We rounded a bend and were mildly surprised to find a large deadfall too low to go under, too high to go over, and too wide to go around. We ended up sloshing our way out onto the bank, carrying most of our stuff through the soupy grass all the way around the top of the dead tree, and then shoving the canoe up and over the huge log. Whew! We were certainly glad *that* was over so we could get on down the river!

An hour later, we had gotten on down the river about a half mile, and we were approaching deadfall number

*Fred cutting away limbs on a deadfall on the
Minago River so that we could get the canoe over it.*

five. Shortly after that, we began to see a winsome variety
of deadfalls and beaver dams. Several times, we encountered overgrowth so thick we had to get out on the bank to
search for the river on the other side of it. When we finally
found where the water came out of the brush, we had to
carry the canoe and gear to it. Often we would both search
for a path through the spiked pine saplings. A couple of
times, when Fred was carrying the canoe, he actually relied
on me—Ms. Guided, who can't find her way out of a den-
tist's office—to steer him through and around to the other
side. I was terrified that I'd dead-end us in that labyrinth.
We had no energy to spare for retracing poorly chosen
routes.

On one trek through the woods, Fred was carrying the

canoe, and I was in front with a pack. The path Fred had to follow with the eighteen and a half feet of Kevlar over his head was quite limited and frustrating to negotiate. He was depending on me to lead him on the path of least resistance. I was not only having trouble finding the way we had gone before, but I also was walking a bit too far ahead for him to see me from under the hull of the canoe. He finally called out, "Joyce, which way do I go?"

"Over here," I said.

He tried to turn the canoe toward the sound of my voice and got hung up a time or two in overhead branches. "Where are you?" he shouted, rather emphatically I noticed.

"Over here."

His voice took on a slight rasp and sounded as if it was coming from between clenched teeth.

"Where in the hell is *'over here'!*" he said.

There were a few more hits and misses before we saw the light at the end of the portage, but eventually we were at the water's edge again. Sometimes we rode, sometimes he walked and I rode. Sometimes we both walked. Sometimes I walked and fell and froze. Sometimes long-legged husband of mine would pull the canoe so fast from the front that I would lose my grip. It was a toss-up as to whether I was helping the canoe along more than it was helping me. We pushed and guided the canoe away from boulders just beneath the surface of the murky ice water. The voyageurs and other tripmen must have had a better method than that. After they had traveled over a piece of ground one time, they surely would have cleared it out for the next time. Apparently, no one had been along that old river for several years before we got there.

My feet and legs were freezing. The bandages covering the road blisters on my heels kept coming off. The mosquitoes were thoroughly enjoying the dinner excursion. Ah! Summer vacation!

For seven hours, we sawed limbs off logs so that the loaded canoe could be heaved over. We hacked crooked little trails around brush-covered sections of the tiny creek. Somewhere between eighteen and twenty-five beaver dams later, we came to a large flat rock and a big patch of grass in a bend of the river. It was home for the night. We hung our wet pants on branches, cooked supper, and hit the hay. Actually, that night we slept on a water bed. We discovered that the whole field of grass was floating on watery muck deep down under the roots.

For the next two days, we had some relief from the toil of breaking through. We came out onto a scenic little oval of water called Gravel Lake. Our Saturday evening entertainment consisted of searching the high banks for a campsite. The entertaining part began to diminish on the second time around the lake. We finally decided on a spot at least thirty feet above the water. We were attracted to it by a small game trail leading up the steep bank.

No rocks were nearby to use for a small cooking fireplace. I dug a hole in the mud on the side of the hill for my tiny fire. Fred found a relatively level area for the tent on a narrow ridge. When we were in the midst of setting up camp, a beaver came waddling along his accustomed route. Suddenly realizing that there was some kind of giant nylon monster in his path, he skirted it and made his way farther up the hill. He stopped and looked back. Nothing but trees and grass had been there the last time he had passed that way.

We decided to spend Sunday resting, not because it was the Sabbath but because we were exhausted. A couple of Sundays had completely escaped our notice. But I had kept God so busy during the weekdays with my urgent requests that He deserved weekends off.

Fred fished awhile and caught five or six decent pike. We kept two and ate fried fish for Sunday dinner. That was the best meal we had on the whole trip, including the ones cooked inside.

We studied the map and found that we were only about one-third of the way through the narrow part of the Minago. Up ahead, we speculated, the territory would continue to be ideal for beaver dams and deadfalls to block the narrow waterway.

Our predictions were only partially realized. We didn't encounter as many deadfalls as in pre-Gravel Lake territory, but we came into a stretch of river that was thick with beaver dams. We developed a system. First, Fred would identify it. "Dam!" he would say. Then I would step out of the bow onto it the best I could, considering my limited aptitude for stepping in general. I would pull the canoe up on it with Fred's help, paddling and pushing from behind, until he could step out. With any luck at all, his feet would not go down through the sticks in the dam. Then we would both heave the remainder of the canoe across. Fred would steady it while I scrambled over the gear to the bow. He would get in and shove off, only to repeat the process less than thirty feet downstream. We did this over and over again.

Finally, the river widened and we had some relief for about eight or nine miles. My leg muscles were sore from the stretching and crawling. Fred never says much about soreness, but I could tell he was tired. I had humongous blisters on my heels. They were third-generation sores left over from the long walk on the road. They had been born again during the trek down in the river bed when my wet socks had rubbed against my sore heels inside my boots.

A strange bright light had glowed in the sky nearly all

day. It seemed to give off a kind of warmth. I vaguely remembered something like that from a time long ago, back
when I was young. I believe it was the day before this trip
started. The paddling was only moderately difficult, and
the wind didn't get up until the last three hours of travel.
We ate lunch on a big flat rock. It was part of the pre-Cam-
brian shield, Fred informed me. All I know is, it was hard
enough that my feet didn't sink into it up to my ankles,
and it was level enough to set a water bottle on without its
toppling into the lake. It was the swankiest lunch spot
we'd found in days.

We moved along fairly well for several more hours
than I would have liked, but we were on a roll and didn't
want to spoil the magic. We came out onto Hill Lake. It was
one of the most appropriately named lakes in the North
Country. It looked as if it could have been a huge hill into
which a deep hole had been dug and filled halfway up
with water. The sides were all hill, steep and muddy. We
spent a long night clinging to one of those sides where we
"pitched" our tent. If it hadn't been for the hordes of
mosquitoes pinning us to the ground, we would probably
have slid off into the lake. From then on, we used that
campsite as comparative criteria:

"Let's try this spot for the tent. It can't be as unlevel as
the one on Hill Lake."

Or, "That was some campsite! All those rocks! And the
mosquitoes were wicked! Almost as bad as Hill Lake!"

RELIEF FROM THE ROUGH

We'll have a chance
To dry our pants
And shoes and socks and persons.
We'll do okay
Another day,
Unless the river worsens.

But for tonight,
We'll be all right;
We'll rest and cook and eat;
An itch we'll scratch,
And find a patch
For blisters on our feet.

On water bed
I'll lay my head
And aching arms and legs.
Day is done,
And I, for one,
Sleep well on soft muskeg.

The dams and logs
And swampy bogs,
I hope are all elsewhere,
Instead of in
Our way again;
I don't need more gray hair!

Cheeseburgers
In Paradise

Drunken Lake was apparently named because of its irregular shape. Weatherworn slabs of white stone lined the shores on all sides. Many small rock islands decorated the lake. A lovely place for a campsite or even a picnic. But, as usual, when the place presented itself, time didn't allow us to take advantage of it. So we pushed on to our next venture, Cross Lake.

Fred's idea was to stop very briefly at the Cross Lake Indian reserve to learn a few details about Pipestone Lake and maybe buy a bag of Paulin's cookies to sustain us until THE END. My ambitions, on the other hand, consisted of sleeping in a bed with clean sheets, and soaking in hot baths. I wanted to eat real food prepared by clean human hands instead of the shredded cardboard reconstituted by my calloused, smoke-blackened fingers.

Unscrupulous freeze-dried food manufacturers have made fortunes by carefully packaging and falsely labeling as food such materials as crumbled drywall, grated woodchips, pressed styrofoam and rabbit pellets. Fred and I have provided these charlatans with at least one of those fortunes. They prey on the innocent backpacker who is so conscious of having to carry everything on his back that he'll buy anything under eight ounces. Once he is three days out, who's he gonna call? And when he gets back, the taste of styrofoam is washed away by that first soft drink, and the rabbit pellets are negated by a quarter-pounder with onions. Occasionally, I ran across a meal that slightly resembled the item after which it was named, providing I cooked it four times as long as the package directed.

Fred had been lodge-shy since our wind-bound prison term at Moose Lake. With no little difficulty, I managed to elicit a vague commitment from him that. possibly he would just ask if there might be some place like a hotel where we could spend the night, if we wanted to.

Signs of civilization began to crop up. First, rooftops began to materialize in the distance. Then we began to see whole houses and even people, the first we'd seen in at least a week.

There were large canoes, with motors, of course. The Indians there would be hard-pressed to paddle a canoe. Why on earth would they use such an antiquated mode of travel when they could have the prestige of owning a fast motorboat! We did see some large canoes being paddled by several pairs of men who were in training for a big canoe race. They had a strange paddling arrangement. The one in front faced the stern and used oars, rowboat-fashion. The stern man seemed to be steering the cumbersome craft with a canoe paddle.

Cross Lake Indian reserve was slightly off-route for us, and we didn't want to go too far in an unprofitable direction. We asked some people along the bank where the main part of town was. They smiled at us, possibly holding back mirthful giggles. They told us it was about two miles and even offered to tow us or take us in their motorboats.

Fred thanked them but said we'd be able to get there under our own steam. I wished he had confined his statement to include only his own steam. My personal supply was sadly depleted.

Whenever we come into a place dog-tired, I always hate it when there are people around. Then I have to spend my very last ounce of strength trying to bring 'er in right smart for our public. But since Fred seems to be able to run on sheer muscle and bone, no matter how sore or overworked those vital body parts might be, we always manage to look much better than I feel.

The village had the usual small store or two, a Hudson's Bay Company store, a pizza place, a video rental place, and the answer to my dreams, a motel. There they served cheeseburgers and fries! Pickles! Onions! It was paradise! Charlie's Inn was run by a true Irishman—Bob. He had lived at the Cross Lake reserve with his Cree wife and eight children for about ten years. He talked with us about how times had changed. He had come from Ireland during the era when the phrase "No Irish need apply" was still quite common around work places. He said the Indians used to take their whole families off to hunting and trapping camps and stay there for long periods of time, especially during the winter. But in the later years, their little houses at the reserve had taken on a more permanent atmosphere because the families were living in them for more months out of the year.

Fred decided he would pack up a few of his camera lenses, his tripod, and several other extra items we had been carrying, and mail them home to get them off our backs. At the small post office, our package weighed in right at fifteen pounds. "Wow!" we told ourselves, "what a relief that was going to be on future portages!" Then we went shopping. We figured we bought about twenty pounds of stuff. Of course, we knew the three pounds of cookies wouldn't last long, and we planned to use the Spork, Canada's answer to Spam, with a pot of beans just as soon as we got time and fuel enough to cook them.

Another important part of our stop-over was to contact the Royal Canadian Mounted Police. They were kind enough to radio the RCMP at The Pas. I can imagine how that communication went:

Cross Lake: We're calling to report the arrival of Fred and Joyce Stone.

The Pas: Who?

Cross Lake: Fred and Joyce Stone. They came here in a canoe.

The Pas: In a canoe? Why?

Cross Lake: Traveling across the province.

The Pas: Oh, yeah?

Cross Lake: They said you wanted them to report in along the way whenever they had the opportunity.

The Pas: We don't even know—Oh, wait a minute. Jack, here, says he thinks he remembers a couple that left here in a canoe about—how many weeks ago, Jack? . . . About eight or ten? . . . He thinks they took off from here at least a couple of months ago. Okay, we'll put it on the record that they were there.

Cross Lake: Right. Thanks.

The Pas: You bet. Have a nice day.

It certainly made me feel safer, knowing we were being monitored so closely. It gave me peace of mind to know that, if something did happen to us "out there," we would be located within a matter of only a decade or two. However, I do have to admit that anyone who goes "out there" should be able to take care of himself or he should stay in town.

I was really surprised when Fred said we'd stay an

extra day in the motel. Of course, talking me into it wasn't easy. He must have begged for at least five seconds.

It was sunny and breezy the morning we resumed our trip. The breeze was especially welcome during our mid-morning snack break because it helped disperse the repulsive odor coming from zillions of dead insect carcasses. Mississippi mud flies, Fred calls them, are huge mosquito-like beings with long frail legs and oval-shaped transparent wings. He reminisced about driving across the Mississippi River toll bridge at Burlington, Iowa, when this same creature was in hatching season. Their carcasses were lying around everywhere, so thick that the highway was almost too slick to drive on. At our rest stop on the lake, waves had plastered the insects on the rocks, and the water was littered with them, creating a gross-looking scum covering the stagnant pools. Eating our snacks in the midst of the stench was not exactly an ideal picnic atmosphere.

Pipestone Lake was beautiful. I still remember its transparent water the color of lime sherbet. I only wish it had stood still long enough for me to appreciate it fully, but it was antagonistic and difficult to deal with as it rolled up under us and shoved us along. It was doubly frustrating because we were having to search about the many islands and points for a way through. Fred had asked several people how to get back to the river. The advice that had some semblance of credibility later turned out to be incredible. The recommended route through Pipestone Lake turned out to be a Pipestone dream. Of course, in all fairness to our informers, the area did have a wide variety of channels and land formations among which it would be easy for canoeists to become disoriented—spelled L-O-S-T! We sorted it out, though, and finally reached the east channel of the Nelson River, where we began paddling *upstream.*

FOOD?

It can't be our supper,
    This grayish-brown glup!
It looks more like something
    Our cat once coughed up!

I see by the label,
    It's something light-weight;
The main problem is—
    It's something I *hate*!

Is dessert in that bag?
    An excellent question.
We'll eat it and flirt
    With gross indigestion!

Here's one that claims
    To be chocolate ice cream.
You gotta be kidding!
    It's just a bad dream.

The potatoes are solid;
    The meat is incredible.
Cooking two hours
    Does not make them edible.

We eat cardboard carrots
    And paperwad peas
And chili con carne—
    Bicarbonate, please!

Can't wait to get back
    To cheeseburgers and fries,
Cholesterol and salt,
    Cellulite on the thighs.

Three burgers I'll order;
    I'll hear the cook shout,
"It'll take half an hour;
    They ain't been thawed out."

Ant
Camp

Even though the current was not strong, by the time we had gone twenty-five miles against it, I was really tired of paddling. Now and then the tiny riffles would quicken, and the canoe would scrape the bottom. I felt that I had improved quite a bit in my paddling skill by that time, but what good was all that proficiency when there wasn't enough water to paddle?

High Hill portage was the only one that had a printed sign on it telling us that we actually were where we thought we were. The sign did not lie. It was a high hill. A crude ladder-like structure ascended the sloping rock. The rungs made from saplings evidently had been designed for hauling large canoes, possibly even small motor boats, up and over the hill. We tried to pull our canoe up it, but there was so much drag that we ended up carrying it, as usual.

Tons of water roared over the falls near the start of the portage. They were powerful, beautiful. At the other end of the path the water was not so pretty. It was thick with mud flies emanating the familiar sewer stench.

Another handful of miles upriver, we arrived at one of

the nicest portages we had encountered on the trip. It consisted of a well-defined walking area across huge stone slabs. My partner made the welcome suggestion that this might be a good campsite. It surely couldn't be any worse than the one on Hill Lake. Or, maybe it could.

Fred found one small squarish piece of earth big enough to accommodate the tent. Shortly after he had our domicile in place, he noticed an intense stinging sensation on his ankle. Then another one on his shin, then another on his calf. Red ants! We had not met them before. It was quite an experience. And when Jaws and his family worked my ankle over, I learned to swat, smack and smash in record time. Once in awhile, I would even hit an ant. So painful were the assaults of the tiny creatures, that no matter what we were doing at the time of the attack, our reflexes would cause us to abandon the activity instantly and move immediately toward eradicating the source of the pain. The sudden bites dangerously cut short such tasks as pouring boiling water into a cup, removing a simmering cooking pot from the campfire, or using only two hands in place of the three that were needed to secure the tent fly before the wind carried it away.

Fred made one of his executive decisions. It would be better to sleep on a sloping hard rock than to spend the night battling an extremely large family of voracious mini-vampires. The tent was moved. Supper was finished. We turned in for the night.

Even at 10:45 P.M., it was still broad daylight, but I had been dead-asleep for an hour when I was jolted awake by the sound of metal clanking against rock.

"Fred!" I whispered as loudly as I could. Why was I whispering? Was I afraid I'd frighten away whatever was out there? I certainly wanted it to be "more afraid of me than I was of it." I guess I wanted it to be there long enough for Fred to see it. Then I wouldn't have to withstand his patronizing look when I tried to describe it to him after it was gone. However, I got no response from the contents of the other sleeping bag. Trying for a tone of horror in my voice that would raise the hair on the back of his neck, I resorted to the Big Four: "THERE'S SOMETHING OUT THERE!" It worked! I only hoped I hadn't scared him too badly.

"Unh?" he grunted, not moving.

I assumed the danger of cardiac arrest was past. I was about to nudge him within an inch of his life, but I hit a snag. I had always thought sleeping bags could be operated by anyone possessing at least the intellect of a pickle. Mine, however, rose up against me with tenacious stubbornness. Making very little progress with the zipper, I struggled to sit up still pinned inside my cocoon. By the time I had wiggled my way over to the tent opening, Fred was sitting cross-legged, quietly gazing through the mosquito netting. Moving through the water was a furry little head making a slowly- widening "V" in the otherwise glassy surface. With a sudden plunk of his tail, the beaver slipped out of sight. He had been snooping around our coffee pot left on the rock slab. The snide little tail-slap probably meant we didn't have anything worth stealing.

Fred crawled back to sleep, but I was wide awake thinking about what lay ahead, what lay behind; which would be the best part, or the worst. I finally became drowsy and started to drift off. Then I thought I heard a familiar sound, faint and far away. *Must be a jet plane up there somewhere,* I tried to convince myself.

"Rumble."

No, I'm not going to let a little "boom" off in the distance keep me awake any longer.

"RUMBLE, RUMBLE."

A thunderstorm. We were lying in a tent held up with metal poles, perched on a large slab of granite, next to a river, out in the open, and we were going to experience a thunderstorm.

"Rumble, rumble. BANG! FLASH! CRASH! Gush, blow. FLASH! BANG!"

Fred finally took notice and then lay there with an interested look on his face. "When there is a span of time between the flash and the crash," he assured me, "the storm is several miles away and not immediately overhead as it appears to be." It was close enough for me.

Somehow the storm didn't eat us alive, but it did tenderize me a great deal. After a couple of hours of exhausted sleep, I opened my eyes to daylight. I was amazed to find that most parts of my body were still in working condition. So I carefully selected a favorite old camping expression: WHADANIGHT!

STORMY WEATHER

Rumble! Rumble!
    The sky's a-tumble
        With wind and lightning and noise!

Heavy rain splashes,
    Hard thunder crashes;
        I nearly lose my poise!

The storm moves on,
    All traces gone;
        Except my knuckles white.

I hope for sleep,
    Some rest to reap.
        Please, no more turmoil tonight!

Can You Say "Echimamish"?

We wound our way up the east arm of the Nelson and came into the Echimamish River. After a few gentle miles, we met the wind on Hairy Lake. It blew us relentlessly in all the wrong directions.

Our newest haven of rest was a pleasant one, an island on Hairy Lake. This little body of water had been named for its "green hair" poking up through the shallow water. The wind was still a little stiff, but that got rid of the mosquitoes. We found an old wooden sled, weather-bleached to a silver gray and held together by hand-cut wooden pins. It probably had been pulled by dogs. Useful to us even in its current state, it made a fine drying rack for our laundry. The evening was easy, and the sun actually followed us to sleep without being intimidated by rain clouds. In the morning, we would take a short portage into the river again.

Almost every night in the tent, we would tape record as much of the day's experience as we could remember, or at least the parts we wanted to remember. Later, when we played the tapes back, a few parts of them were more in-

A view from our tent of Hairy Lake.
The green weeds poking up through the shallow water
resemble fine hair.

teresting than we could have imagined. The words we had recorded did not stimulate our memories and reawaken our pleasure nearly as much as the background noises— the sound of the water as the canoe rippled through it, the paddle being dipped and retrieved and occasionally brushing the side of the canoe, bird calls that we never hear in Indiana, and the cries of gulls, ravens, and our beloved loons.

The tape recordings also captured intonations in our voices that we hadn't counted on. It caught the tears in my voice when I spoke about a nephew just out of high school who lay in a coma from an auto accident. It picked up the depression in Fred's voice when we were wind-bound in the lodge and couldn't move for several days. It rolled through several feet of insignificant details about this wilderness experience in which we had invested our souls. It reviewed the giggles we shared over the Flying Beaver. It reproduced the dwindling optimism as day after day went by while we hunted the headwaters of the Minago River.

One humorous thread that wove in and out of the recorded entries for a week or more was our changing pronunciation of one of our favorite rivers—the Echimamish. We were surprised at the number of ways the people in Manitoba said the word *Echimamish*. Looking at the map at home, we had taken a wild shot at the pronunciation. Along the trip route, hardly anyone seemed to know that it existed until we got close to the river itself near Cross Lake. The people at the Indian reserve there rattled off some Cree phrases at one another. I could hear the name go by now and then as they spoke.

The meaning of the name has to do with the fact that the current in the river changes directions abruptly. It flows the opposite way when it reaches a high spot. There, the water is forced to make a decision on whether it wants to head out toward Hudson Bay, the way we were going, or end up back in Lake Winnipeg and take an alternate route to the Bay. The Cree word seems to correspond with the English phrase "each way." The *each* probably is derived from *Echi*. A loose interpretation of it, with which not everyone agrees, is "river that runs two ways." It has also been called Each-a-way mak mus Brook, Eachaway Mans Brook, and one or two equally colorful mispronunciations of our own creation.

We both became so confused in trying to change the word to something in keeping with the origin of it that we botched it up most of the time. When we played back that portion of the tape we made while traveling on the river itself, we heard ourselves pronouncing it hesitantly and a bit differently each day. Nearing the end of the Echimamish stretch of the river, Fred made one last attempt at the name. On the tape, it came out, "Ech—, Ek—, Eshama—, . . . (small sigh) . . . the RIVER!"

We were still paddling uphill, but the water was smooth and the current languid. We came to the remains of an old dam made of vertical logs sticking up about a foot and a half above the surface of the water. We had been told by Bob back at Cross Lake that several dams had been built to increase the depth of water for the forty-two-foot York boats. These vessels carried nine thousand pounds of cargo and a crew of nine. There were two hundred York boats manned by 1,200 tripmen in the Hudson's Bay Company. The boats were constructed at York Factory, originally. They were built with sides about six inches thick to withstand rugged treatment on portages and rapids. The one we saw later at Lower Fort Garry reminded me of a thick wooden salad bowl. It was difficult to imagine the heavy boats being paddled and portaged over some of the places we had been.

Riel Berard has made several sets of maps that outline various canoe routes. The maps are twenty-one by thirty inches and are almost completely covered with information about the routes. Particularly interesting are drawings of artifacts, symbols, pictographs, and animals that are related in some way to the routes. Even the explorers and famous settlers of those areas are pictured, along with their brief biographical sketches. He has included excerpts from journals of people who helped open the waterways for the fur trade. Most of the information about good places to camp, the length of portages, and the location and suggestions for the best approach to rapids seem to be based on Berard's own experience. I carried the Middle Track and

Hayes River Route map in a plastic Hudson's Bay store bag and pored over it nightly to see what was in store for me the next day. I finally had to tape it together at the worn folds. There is a note of caution printed on the maps saying that the information was gathered more than twenty-five years ago, and that the charts should be used in conjunction with current topographical maps. We found only a small error or two in the exact number of rapids that were safe to run and in the location of one landmark. Even if the maps are not used as the sole source of information for a canoe trip, they are fascinating to read on a winter's evening when one needs to dream about the summer ahead. They do for canoeists what seed catalogs do for gardeners: give shape to our dreams.

The large rock slab over which we carried the gear at Painted Stone Portage. The river flowed in the opposite direction on the other side of the rock.

The point where the Echimamish changes directions occurs at the Painted Stone Portage. This place is a large expanse of stone. The portage from one side of it to the other is about 100 feet. According to our Berard map, the Indians at one time had a kind of worshipping place on that spot. Berard said there was a large stone at which they placed offerings. They also painted symbols on the stone. When the fur traders began coming through, it was evidently impossible to carry the York boats and gear around this edifice, and so it was taken away. In spite of the fact that the fur trade with the Indians was the main inspiration for the settlement of the North Country, the greed for money from the furs had wiped out the Indian relic that marked a river that ran two ways.

We camped at the Painted Stone Portage. It was grossly obvious that other parties had camped there over a span of many years. A variety of garbage littered the area, typical of what we found in a handful of the more heavily traveled areas. Such trashiness is out of place in an urban area, let alone in the middle of a wilderness. It had probably been at least a year or more since the stuff had been left. Rusting and half-burned cans, broken beer bottles, and mutilated plastic containers were strewn about. People had taken things out there that I would never even carry from the house to the car. It was unfortunate that the place was such a mess because it was one of the most level camp sites we had used. It had breezy, open areas and was also close to the water. The feeling of the ancient past was nearly gone, though. There were too many jarring modern-day vibrations about the place, such as "George was here, July, 1980."

Breakfast with the mosquitoes was interesting. They were so thick around the place we could hardly keep them out of our mouths. When I tried to refry some leftover pancakes, mosquitoes fell into the pan and were cooked, too. Oh well, I suppose it was better than eating them raw. And someday I might even become famous for the recipe. I could call them McMosquito Cakes.

SPEECH IMPEDIMENT

Tape recordings
  Are terrible!
    Revealing and ruthlessly real!

We talk and talk,
  But rarely come forth
    With any cerebral appeal.

Our shallow thoughts
  We often express
    In stammering speech so inept;

The world would be
  Much better off
    If vows of silence we kept!

Ledge Leaping

Downhill, finally! The current had reversed itself just as the literature about the Painted Stone had promised. Next we had to psych ourselves up for the portage at the end of Robinson Lake. It had been rumored to be anywhere from just over a mile to five miles long. We paddled the lake in good style and found the portage easily.

The Robinson Portage was the most interesting walk of all. There were remains of barrels and parts of an old railway for carts that had been used to haul gear, trade goods, and fur packs over the hill. Litter! But original litter. I have concluded that it is less obnoxious than modern litter only because of its historical value. When I thought about carrying the glass jar or the Spork can across all those portages, it was difficult not to give in to temptation and leave it beside the cast-off junk of others who had gone before. But I didn't.

The litter at the Robinson Portage was a reminder of the hundreds of packs of trade goods that must have been hauled across it. On Berard's map, one of the notes he makes reads as follows:

White or Robinson, Falls; portage 1800 paces, Franklin mentions of seeing a Lobstick here at the portage and adds, "I shall long remember the rude and characteristic wilderness of the scenery which surrounded these falls; rocks piled on rocks hung in rude and shapeless masses over the agitated torrents which swept their bases, whilst the lichens that covered the faces of the cliffs, contrasting with the dark green pines which crowned their summits." October 2, 1819. On the evening of August 11th 1910, Earl Grey, then Governor General of Canada and on official visit from Norway House to York Factory, camped at Robinson Falls by the tramway line.

We had braced ourselves for a long carry. The trail did cross a "quality" hill and valley near the end. But walking the length of it double took us only an hour and a half, much less time than expected. I took a photograph of Fred coming down the big hill with the canoe. As usual, the camera minimized the steepness of the hill because of the angle from which the picture had to be shot.

The trail itself was clear. Compared to the territory we had slogged, waded, and chopped our way through, it was a super highway. Another of Fred's Favorites fit pretty well: "It's wide enough to drive a semi across." It ran parallel to an indentation we thought was probably the original walking trail. Long rusty strips of metal lay beyond that. The old tramway must have been located in that vicinity. Carts used for portaging the furs and gear had somehow been rolled along the rails. To one side of the trail, we saw an axle with its two rail wheels still attached. Those guys knew how to haul their freight!

Since that time, I have seen an old picture of the portage area in which tents and camping paraphernalia were situated around the end of the tramway near the portage trail. The efficiency and productivity of the fur-trade operation would probably have boggled our minds.

We thought we had a good supply of modern equipment and enough experience to go with it, but we were mere children in the wilderness compared to the people who were there first. Most of them were men, but there were several women, either tough old gals who could handle anything or coddled ladies who had to be taken care of by the underlings in order to survive. I wondered which type I would have been if I had lived under those circumstances.

A few more portages, a bit more river, and we arrived at Logan Lake. The campsite we found was ideal for a real home. Evidently someone else had thought so, too. A square of logs was laid out for the beginnings of a cabin. Small bushes growing up inside it indicated that it had been given up several years before. The point of land jutting out into the lake had all the picture-postcard trimmings. Aesthetically-balanced pines, spruce trees, and juniper bushes accented the slab of pink rock where it met the water. Sunlight filtered through the huge pines in the forest behind us.

We slept indoors, so to speak. Fred put the tent in the middle of the house frame, since it was the most level area. During the night, it was proven to me that our tent could not be blown away with us inside it. When we had gone to bed that evening, the sun had been shining. Everything had been dry and clear. It would surely be that way in the morning; I could get by just this once without putting anything over the firewood to keep it dry, couldn't I?

The treetops began thrashing just after dark. Wind blowing through pine trees is comparable to water flowing over a shallow bed of rocks. It sounds more ferocious than it really is. Since my mind usually improves on ferocity tenfold, what surprised me most when I woke up the next morning was that I had gone to sleep during the storm. I crawled out of the tent to rain-soaked firewood and general sogginess everywhere.

I tried really hard to get a fire going and even had it once or twice, but then lost it. In order to beat the wind, we finally moved out without any breakfast, which didn't help our tolerance for the threatening skies and long portages ahead, or even for each others' irritating little habits. On one of the portages, we did pause long enough to get a small fire going. Hot soup and cereal brightened the day considerably.

On downstream, we surprised a cow moose having breakfast. About 8:00 A.M., we came around a bend, and there she was, standing shoulder-deep in the water. She didn't see us for a few seconds, and I was able to shoot a picture or two. When she finally did realize there was something unusual entering her environment, she just stood there looking at us, a big string of grass she'd pulled up from the river bottom hanging out of her mouth. Finally, in mid-chomp, she decided she'd better leave. She just couldn't trust that long yellow thing floating on the water!

The river widened, making the riffles barely visible up ahead. The noise usually warned us, but we came upon one quiet set that looked tame until we got within a couple of canoe lengths. Sitting about nine feet closer to the rapids than Fred, I was suddenly treated to a breath-taking view of water pouring over a four-foot drop. I felt moved to describe the scene in loud panicky screeches: "It's a LEDGE! Back paddle!"

Then from nine feet south of me came words I considered to be extremely depressing and even in bad taste: "It's too late! Straighten 'er up! We're goin' over it."

Fred was right. We did. But by some quirk of fate, we were successful. Later reflections on the incident were spiced with comments such as, "Man! I couldn't even see it until we were on top of it!"

"I don't know how you did it, but if you hadn't brought the canoe around straight, we'd have been pickin' up gear for weeks."

"Well, I just leaned back as far as I could, and somehow the water didn't come over the side."

Of course, a Sunday jag down through a rock garden and over a few ledges probably wouldn't even raise the pulse rate of a solo canoeist wearing a wet-suit and paddling a covered canoe. But to a bow paddler in the middle of a cold river on a wilderness trip, thoughts were not about how much exhilaration would be in store for us, but whether we would be able to salvage enough gear to finish the trip, or at least stay alive for awhile.

There was another time, though, that I could have leaned myself into a backbend, and the huge frothing hole we dived into would still have swooshed several gallons of water into the canoe. We were into another set of rapids that didn't look really threatening until we were right at the edge of them. To avoid some of the real bruisers, we had tried to paddle across the current. It was running a little faster than we had judged, and suddenly we were being plummeted toward a large pit churning with white water. Fred said, "Lean back! We're going to punch it!"

I learned that the words "punch it" have extremely negative connotations, such as cold, wet shoes and pants and shirt, and sizeable loss of control of a floating tanker one-third full of water. The water inside the boat rolled us slightly from side to side. It would have taken but one little gesture to throw us off balance, and we'd have bought the river! We managed to ease the boat over to the bank. Then we had the job of returning the water to the place from whence it came. We used a plastic bleach bottle Fred had very professionally converted into a bailer for the trip. It wasn't exactly hypothermia time, but it was too chilly that morning for me to stand around in wet garments. I finally had to change clothes.

Then another phenomenon occurred. The map had indicated a long set of rapids extending around a bend. We stopped at the beginning of the fast water and climbed the high banks. We scrambled up and down hills, through brush and briars, until we came to a point where we could see almost the whole curve. What we saw appeared to be no more than just fast water, something we were a bit familiar with by that time. The signs were all good. We elected to paddle through it and take a chance on the one little area we couldn't see. We knew better than to take such a risk. It was not the mark of experienced paddlers, but we were so tired! No horror stories here, though. We did it easily. The one little blind spot turned out to be even quieter than the rest. Piece of cake! (Piece of *luck!*)

Windy Lake kept its promise. It was, indeed. But then, so was every lake we'd encountered en route. We camped on a point and tried to hide from the wind down behind a gigantic split rock. Even the next morning, I was having trouble keeping a match lit long enough to start a fire. So again, we postponed breakfast and took off. We paddled the rest of the lake with no further difficulty and stopped to eat a bite just before leaving it. The wind settled down a bit, and the morning showed real promise. We came across a few more mild rapids, but nothing that could ruin the day.

LOVELY LEDGES

I've looked at lots of lovely ledges
   Over guard rails made of steel,
Built to keep me safe from water
   That would grind me into meal.

We traveled far to get to places
   Left unguarded by the State.
Guard rails, caution signs were absent;
   None to warn us of our fate.

No protection were we given,
   But to make our own defense
Against that river wild and swift;
   We called on judgment, common sense.

I've looked at lots of leaping water
   Pouring over steep incline.
Whose canoe is heading toward it?
   Could that boat be his and *mine?*

I've plied my paddle sideways, backwards;
   Paddling forward wouldn't do it.
"Straighten up! You'll miss that boulder,"
   Fred would say. "There's nothin' to it!"

Had I not been tired each night,
   Lots of sleep I would have lost,
Thinking of impending upsets—
   How much all our gear had cost!

So I was glad we strained and sweat;
   My sanity it helped me keep.
Much too tired to think of ledges,
   I'd fall into weary sleep.

And thanks to ledges on that river,
I will my perspective keep
On what my life has yet to offer;
All its ledges I can leap.

Crossing Oxford Lake

The wind was down. The sun was up. The tremolo of a loon drifted across the lake. All was right with the world. At least, for the moment.

We stopped for lunch at a large outcropping of granite. I lay back on the big slab of rock and let the sun warm my face. It felt *wonderful*. The blue sky was *wonderful*. The smooth water was *wonderful*. My partner was *wonderful!* Something had to be terribly *wrong!*

The half hour spent nourishing body and soul in that pleasant spot passed quickly. Back on the river, I was inspired to hum a tune while I snapped a few pictures. I had to admit to myself that it was rather nice to paddle with a strong partner, however unfair he might have seemed at times. One slight flaw in his character was his inability to realize that I, a nature lover, needed to pause occasionally in the daily drudgery. My artistic soul needed time to drink in the vast beauty. He seemed to think that I should dip my paddle quite a bit more frequently and with a great deal more energy than I felt entirely necessary. He was expecting too much of me. It was almost as if he thought *I* should paddle as much as *he* did!

But for that moment, everything was still fine. Up ahead, the river widened into a lake. Oxford Lake, about forty-five to fifty miles long, would be one of the largest lakes we would cross on this trip. The water looked fairly smooth, just a few tiny ripples across the surface. Then, the sun disappeared. But it was hidden for only a moment by a fluffy little white cloud. No problem! Besides, the light breeze that had just passed over was coming from behind us. Maybe we could put our paddles down and just sail across the lake as the voyageurs did. They carried a sail in their canoes and would hoist it at opportune times. I thought a large raincoat might be a good substitute. It always seemed to catch the wind when it was blowing against us. I tried holding mine up, but I learned that not only would a real sail have been much more efficient, a real mast is a must. So I gave up my labor-saving invention. Too much work!

The best thing to do, we agreed, was to stay close to the shoreline, as usual. But all those huge inlets and bays outlined on the map meant we would eventually have to make some decisions. We would either have to paddle like crazy across the open water for at least three or more miles at one hitch or work our way laboriously around the inside of the bays, traveling three or four times as far. We were well aware that wind and weather could change drastically on the surface of a long open stretch of water in no time flat. But we also remembered fighting wind-driven waves that kept shoving us closer and closer to a shoreline strewn with jagged rocks. If we had tried to reach the safety of land only a few feet away, we would have run the risk of having our canoe and gear dashed to bits.

We hadn't come to the large open part yet, but as the lake stretched out before us, the little breeze began tickling its way across the big water, leaving large ruffled patches off in the distance. We saw no cause for worry. They faded away quickly. The light wind whipped across my back, and I suddenly needed to put on something with long sleeves. The sun deserted us completely. Fifteen minutes later, the wind had sharpened and was teasing the old lake into a frenzy of little whitecaps. Those soon began to give way to two- and three-foot rollers.

At some point between the little whitecaps and the big rollers, the canoe started lurching and leaping into the air and then crashing back into the water. I began to cancel the previous *"wonderful's"* including the one about my partner. He was beginning to say really disgusting things like, "Hey! Isn't this fun! We're surfin'!"

I couldn't even reach the water with my paddle half of the time! Did he notice? *No!* My not-too-gentle inquiries of concern brought patronizing answers like, *"No,* we are *not* going to take on any water. I'm watching behind me. All I have to do is lean the right direction at the right time! Now, *paddle!* We'll be across this before you know it."

My buttocks clung to the seat of the bucking canoe, and I tried to quit grabbing the gunwales to keep my balance. Then the former Mr. Wonderful provided me with the perfect motive for justifiable homicide. He said, "This would make a great picture! Why don't you shoot a few?"

For a moment, I tried to figure out to whom he could be addressing that insane request. Then I thought, *Oh, now I get it! He's joking.* I contemplated the poor timing and tastelessness of his sick humor, until it dawned on me that he was serious! He really expected me to loosen my death grip on the paddle and extract my camera from the tightly-sealed waterproof bag. Then he assumed I would aim, focus, and snap a picture of that turmoil! I knew that was the kind of *shooting* he meant, but for one wild moment, my thoughts drifted dangerously toward another, more personally satisfying kind. I managed to break the weld between my fingers and the paddle. I braced myself the best I could with my knees against the sides of the canoe. I even tried to put my paddle in a safe place, just in case I would ever need it again.

Getting a camera out of a bag usually poses very little threat during peace-time, but now that we were at war with Mother Nature, the camera and the bag both seemed to be on her side. They put up a healthy battle, but I emerged victorious, actually managing to shoot several fast frames between the swayings and the lurchings. (Later, when we saw the prints from this episode, we appreciated the wide selection. There was a nice one of Fred—looking rugged and satisfied, loving every minute of his battle with the waves. There was also a slanty one of just the waves, a well-framed close-up of my knee, a detailed shot of the floor of the canoe, and two well-focused ones of the sky.)

I hastily returned the camera to its bag and gave it a toss, hoping it would land in a relatively-dry spot on the floor. I retrieved the paddle, and my fingers slid easily back into the grooves I had previously squeezed into the wooden shaft. I began slashing away at whatever water I could reach. While high atop the crest of a roller, I made a casual inquiry concerning our destination: "Where're we goin'?"

Fred shouted back, "See that point just up ahead there?"

I aimed my finger hopefully at a small piece of land sticking out from a distant shoreline.

"Yeah. Now, see the one beyond that?"

I nodded dismally and adjusted my aim.

"No, not the big island. It's the point beyond *that*."

I moved my finger a bit farther and stared in disbelief at a tiny jut of land barely visible on the misty horizon.

"Yeah, that's it. I'd say it's about five or six miles straight across there," he said.

"Five or six miles!" My high-pitched yelp was lost in the wind.

He responded with a vague, "Uh-huh."

"We'll never make it!" I said. "The wind's changing directions and starting to come at us from the side!"

"No, we probably *won't* make it if you don't put your paddle in the water!" said my partner.

So, I paddled—and paddled—and *paddled!*

"How much farther now?" I shrieked.

"About five or six miles."

"That's what you said twenty minutes ago!"

"It was *five* minutes ago! *paddle!*"

The canoe really was making good time, but I didn't think about it much because I was pretty busy grabbing at one wave while trying to estimate the time of arrival of the next without looking back. I knew it was going to be a close race between our landing on that speck in the distance and the complete failure of my heart.

Then Fred made a funny little noise, "Uh?" The power was completely gone from the stern. The canoe went almost dead in the water. I wasn't alarmed for a few seconds. I just thought he had stopped to put suntan lotion on or something.

Then I heard, "Well I'll be damned!"

That was my cue. "What's the matter?"

"My paddle just broke!"

I was able to turn my head just enough to see the paddle bent almost double at the point where it joined the shaft. He quickly switched to the spare paddle, but the broken one had been the light-weight, streamlined luxury model. Its breaking was a sour note.

Eons later, I began to notice that our goal had become slightly larger. I took up a more vigilant scanning of the vague outline ahead. Eventually, trees emerged as separate units. A mere thousand or so paddle strokes later, the larger rocks became distinct. Other things on the shore were becoming life-sized instead of dollhouse miniatures. During this gradual return to reality, my uneasiness, insecurity, and fear were watered down by irritation, fatigue, and disgust! I was torn between a feeling of weak-kneed relief that I was going to survive the ordeal, and a vicious, self-deprecating wish that I had drowned so that I could stare a glassy-eyed "I-told-you-so" at my partner. After my death, I would have haunted this man and seen to it that he went through life as a wretched, guilt-ridden solo paddler. Of course, by that time, he might have preferred to be a solo paddler. Wouldn't that have been a bummer!

We finally set foot on solid ground, but there was so much dashing and thrashing of wind and waves all around us on the little point that it seemed almost as if we were camping on the surface of the lake. The campsite was one that had been used not too many months before, probably by the Cree Indians from Oxford Lake several miles ahead of us. They evidently had set up a fishing or trapping camp. A few partially burned pieces of firewood and some blackened stones were indications of a fireplace. A frame made from saplings had evidently been used as a fish-drying rack.

The wind didn't subside for hours. We turned the canoe on its side for a windbreak in order to start a small cooking fire. There were plenty of stones and a large open space all around it. No danger of it spreading. We were always extremely careful about that.

Each task was an enormous effort for exhausted muscles. Even eating was a chore, but I needed the nourishment, and afterward, I did feel more human and less like a dishtowel that had been through the heavy-duty spin cycle.

Finally, in the tent, I relaxed and listened to the waves still crashing on the rocks a few feet away. My inner ear hadn't realized yet that I was on solid ground. Even though I lay still, the sand beneath the tent continued to undulate.

Just as sleep was beginning to take me away, a tiny nagging sensation began needling me. The shock almost reawakened me. I was actually beginning to feel a tinge of pride because I had been able to stay with it out there. And, it got worse! I was experiencing a strange kind of misplaced gratitude toward my partner for making me do what I might not have been able to make myself do. *Well,* I thought, *I'm certainly* (yawn) *not going to admit it* (sigh) *right away. Maybe I'll mention it in a couple of days* (yawn) *or months . . . . I do hope I got at least one or two good pictures.*

FUN FOR FRED—Not Fun For Joyce!

What's that tiny dot up there?
Oh, that's where we are going, Dear.

It's so FAR, we won't arrive
For hours! *If we stay alive!*

Less talk, more paddling. Just don't quit.
This bouncing seat won't let me sit!

How 'bout gettin' a snapshot of this?
You're kidding! With all of this motion, I'd *miss!*

Just like surfin'! Ain't this a ball!
Where are your marbles? Have you lost them all!

Pipe down and paddle; we're gettin' closer.
If we get there, I'm *not leavin'!* NO-sir!

Oxford
House

I'd had it with the wind. I really resented being tumbled, tossed, and pushed around against my will. Even The Surfer was getting pretty sick of it. We decided to get up the next morning just before dawn. And that wasn't easy. In July on Oxford Lake, the night sky begins paling in the northeast around 3:45 A.M. By about 4:30, the sun has rudely spilled its light all over the sleeping Northworld.

We left in semi-darkness. Light fog hovered just above the flat murky water. Pine-tree islands poked up through the mist. When the edge of the sun appeared, the smooth water became a burnished gold mirror.

We paddled much faster than was necessary across the broad expanses between the islands, but for once, the extra hard work seemed logical to me. Beating the wind across Oxford Lake was high on my list of priorities.

In a while, we began to see rooftops and then the usual trucks, cars and people. Whoa! Let's replay that. Cars? Trucks? How could that be? There were no roads into the place from the outside world.

We came around a point, and there, sprinkled casually around the cove, were the buildings of Oxford House—the Bay store, the nursing station, a post office, a school, a white church with a steeple, and the usual array of small houses. A few sleepy Indian children sat in door sills. It was still only about 7:30.

As we started across the bay, a motorboat came over to us and stopped. The man operating it was an Indian named George Crane. We exchanged a few words about ourselves for some information about the community. He said there was neither a restaurant nor any sleeping quarters for travelers. Fred was not really interested in sleeping there anyhow. He had already established a firm position on spending any more time in a motel, hotel, or lodge. And I thought he just might go on without me if I decided to sleep there. The absence of lodging was a moot point.

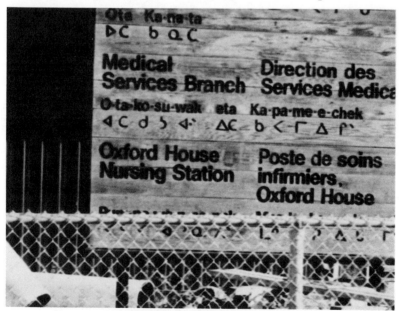

Three types of written language at Oxford House:
French, English, and Cree.

We put in at a dock and climbed up the hill to the nursing station. These medical facilities at the Indian reserves are like small hospitals. People can receive outpatient care or even stay there for a few days, depending on the severity of the illness or injury. If surgery or other more complicated treatment is required, the patients are flown to hospitals in a larger city, sometimes more than half a province away. We thought we could get some further information there about the town and where we could get something to eat that hadn't yet been rendered waterless. We knocked on the door and roused the head nurse from sleep.

Lois Young had been stationed there for three months. Her home was in Newfoundland. I asked if there was some place in town where we could take a shower or clean up somehow. She said there was no place, but she generously offered to let me use a tub in one of the bath rooms at the nursing station. I accepted immediately. Fred looked at me as though I were daft. I had campfire clothes on, and my cleaner ones were deep in the tightly strapped Bill's Bags, down the hill in the canoe. I did have my hip belt containing my comb and toothbrush.

That was the most memorable bath I've ever had. The tub was huge, a hospital version of a jacuzzi. I could float in it! It was probably built for giving people therapy in the water. I filled the tub two-thirds full with water hot enough to boil several layers of epidermis. My sore neglected body settled down into the clean hot water. I laid my head back and soaked my dirty limp hair. Lois had even brought me some of her shampoo. I fondled the big white bar of soap with my sooty hands, cracked and rough from my "vacation" in the wilderness. I dug my dirty fingernails into the bar, and I scrubbed my calloused palms and black knuckles. My body, my hair, and my spirits all revived. There *was* life after canoeing. I am still grateful to Lois and will always associate her name with the luxury of hot water after weeks of cold lakes, cold rain, and cold wind. Feeling like a queen, I donned my ridiculously filthy clothes and met Fred outside. I thanked Lois so profusely that she must have thought I was a real cleanliness nut.

We found out from some of the local people that most of the food and supplies were brought in over a winter road. Other items were flown in by bush plane. When the lakes had frozen to eighteen inches thick, a dozer would clear a specified route across the land and over the lakes. A construction foreman told Fred that sixty semi trailer loads of building supplies had been hauled in to build the government offices and the nursing station. The drivers waited until the ice was thirty inches thick, and then they drove in convoys. They could not go any faster than eight miles an hour across the lakes, and they had to stay a half mile apart. The ice had a certain amount of "give" to it, he said, and it pressed down, causing a kind of wave to push up in front of the trucks and rise up again behind them. He said one fellow tried to go just a little faster—a searing fifteen miles per hour. His truck broke through, and they had to drag it out of twenty-five feet of water. He got out all right, but he lost his job.

We paddled over to the smallest Hudson's Bay store we had seen yet, a metal building that was divided into a grocery store and a dry-goods-hardware store. However, in 1798, Oxford House had been a busy place. The first inland Hudson Bay post had been established there. It was probably bigger then that it is now. We used the phone in the manager's office to call home. He said he would contact the RCMP at Norway House and tell them that the Stones had passed through there. They, in turn, would relay the message to the police at The Pas. We felt sure the RCMP all across Manitoba would be overwhelmed with relief to hear that we were still safe.

We gorged on salami, cheese, bread, mayonnaise, two orange drinks, potato chips, and two chocolate ice cream cones. Our grocery bill amounted to $29.00 in Canadian money, not counting the ice cream and soft drinks.

A young conservation officer we met in the Hudson's Bay store said the portages from there to York Factory ought to be easy to find. He told us the Hayes River was high, and some of the rapids would be better because of it. In other cases they might be more ferocious. I didn't like his choice of words.

We left Oxford House, full of food and growing a bit sleepy due to our arising at 4:00 A.M. We had been on the trip for one month. We were still somewhere around 220 canoe miles from York Factory. But, hey, we were closer than we'd ever seen before!

AH-H-H-H!

Hot water,
    Big tub,
        Towels, soap;
        There is hope!

Pink shampoo,
    Washcloth,
        Hairbrush;
        Don't rush!

Porcelain sink,
    Flushing stool;
        Say no more,
        Close the door!

Clean skin,
    Fluffy hair;
        Feel like new;
        Indeed, I do!

Deep Knee Bends

When choosing the locations for our first few campsites, we had labored under the misconception that the tent must be placed on smooth, level ground. That myth was quickly dispelled by a few desperation campsites where we felt lucky to be able to stretch both bodies out full length. We no longer complained about a little bump under one shoulder or a slight tilt to the pelvis. If we felt the campsite worth mentioning, we compared it with Hill Lake or the Ant Camp or a growing number of other substandard pieces of waterfront property we had used. But there was one we actually had to pass up altogether.

The wind was wearing away at us again. We were beginning a long tussle with it late in the afternoon on big ole' Knee Lake. We were tired, ready to quit for the day. It was one of those times when my eyes routinely scanned the shoreline constantly for a patch of rock, muskeg, sand —anything that came close to being as big as our tent floor. Across a small bay, we spotted a place that looked as if it had possibilities. To reach it, we had to cross about a mile and a half of choppy water with the wind in our faces. Fred got out to do the usual scouting. After a couple of minutes, he said, "You ain't gonna believe this." I climbed out of the canoe and was greeted by at least a half acre of tree stumps.

At first, we thought loggers had leveled the patch of birches, but an inspection of the pointed stakes told us that a beaver had been honing down his teeth. I had heard that beavers' teeth keep growing and must be used constantly to retain a normal size. We were ticked off at old Sharp Tooth. We had been deceived into thinking we had found a cleared spot to camp. The stumps were so close together that there was not room for a tent between them. If the trees had still been attached to them, we could have seen from a distance that the place was no good for a campsite. Then we wouldn't have battled our way across the bay and dragged our weary bodies up there. It was quite a let-down.

After continuing the war with the wind for a while longer, we finally chose a campsite "upstairs." We climbed a thirty-foot rock that was perpendicular to the boulder-strewn shore. When we recovered from hauling all of the gear up the side of the bluff, we were able to think of it as a nice spot. An open expanse of lichen-covered stone over-looked a broad view of Knee Lake which was dotted with fir tree islands. A lovely place for a home.

When we explored the surrounding area, we discov-ered the remains of a large log house. The ax-hewn logs were unusual because of their size. The trees we had been seeing were not nearly that big in diameter. We thought perhaps they had been transported from a few miles away rather than having been cut in the immediate vicinity. The house must have been at least fifteen by twenty feet. The trees growing up inside the framework and the rotted condition of the logs indicated that a great many years had passed since the home was last occupied.

The next morning we started out under threatening skies. We paddled for awhile, but the cold rain came again and blew in our faces, drenching us, body and soul. Fred's raincoat succumbed to its force. His clothes were saturated. He might as well have been wearing a regular cloth coat.

A cunning little deception Knee Lake had in store for us was Magnetic Island. We had read about the reef containing magnetic iron ore in its stone, so both of us were watching our respective compasses glued in the floor of the canoe in front of our respective feet. Mine had been put there by my partner to keep me from constantly bugging him about which direction we were going. When we neared the bend of the "knee," the needles swung around to the opposite direction. That phenomenon probably had caused more than one guide to break out in a cold sweat. But Sir John Franklin knew about it even in 1819. I'm glad he didn't keep it a secret.

Besides learning to use anything short of a body of water for a campsite, we began to adjust to a variety of adverse weather conditions. We found that Nature always deals and the dealer always wins. I remember the times of catharsis—ranting, raving, and ugly threats thrown skyward. These occurred mostly after battles with wind, waves, rain, rapids, or muskeg. Sometimes Fred even joined in.

We welcomed the wind at our backs when it eased the strain of paddling, and we hid from it behind islands and high banks when it blew in our faces and refused to relent. For a while, the twin sounds of water rushing over rocks and of wind blowing through the trees were so similar that they were confusing to us. We came to realize that a continuous, unvarying hiss is caused by water flowing steadily over an obstruction. But the sound of the wind rustling in the trees is not constant. It rises and subsides. Fred also found that he had the power to make clouds cover the sun. He simply stripped down to his swim trunks to feel its warmth, and bingo! It was gone.

We finally stopped for lunch. Sheets of rain were still coming down. There was never any shelter from it. At the end of a canoe trip, the thing I always appreciate most is hot water at the twist of a handle. The second best thing is being able to get in out of the rain. Nature has nothing to offer, short of a cave, to protect a person from water falling out of the sky.

For whatever relief it might afford, I stood beneath the branches of a sparse evergreen tree. But there was as much water coming off of its tossing branches as there was rain coming out of the sky. I pulled some bread out of the bag, trying not to let any water penetrate the protective wrapping. The rain poured harder. Was that the kind of punishment I could look forward to at the end of my life for being bad? I began to regret all the terrible things I'd done. It was too late to confess to my teacher about copying one of the answers on my fourth grade geography test, but I might try to stop being so critical of others. And I could at least make an effort not to call my husband bad names on certain occasions. I had always thought Hell was hot and dry. But maybe things are reversed for canoeists. Maybe Heaven is hot and dry. I could live with that!

I wondered if I could move quickly enough to prevent the entire contents of the lunch bag from becoming soaked while I exhumed the peanut butter and jelly. The real test of dexterity would come when I attempted to apply the spreads to the bread before it reverted to the stage of watery dough. But as I probed the lunch bag experimentally, things took a slight turn for the better. My fingers latched onto a *can!* I withdrew it and read "potted meat" on the label. No mixing, easy to spread! God had let up on me for a moment. *Good. Now I'll just rip the tab top off and—Rats! Gotta have a can opener. Okay, you little miracle knife. This is your chance to live up to the boasts of the man at the knife store. Open this can!* Punch! Poke! *Aw, c'mon! Gimme a break!*

Somehow, wet hands barely able to hold onto a wet knife and a wet can, managed to get the lid open enough to dig out the contents. The most vivid memory I have of the whole event is when I bent my hooded head over the bread to protect it from rain while I spread the meat on it. Rain ran off my hood in rivulets around the lunch I was holding. The sandwiches were beginning to droop down the sides of my hands. The scene looked like a painting by Salvadore Dali.

Fred finished securing the canoe. Out of the corner of my eye, I saw him walking slowly toward me. He came close enough to see the way my jaw was set. After peering at me from under the dripping brim of his hat for a minute, he said with pseudo gaiety in his voice, "Well, Honey, it just doesn't get any better than this!"

I am seldom at loss for a quick laugh. Ordinarily, my sense of humor surfaces at the least suggestion, often getting me in big trouble. But how dare he think that bizarre situation was funny! I certainly hadn't found anything amusing in it, and he was probably colder and wetter than I was, due to the failure of his goretex raincoat hours before. For once, his wit made *me* want to strangle *him*, instead of vice versa.

We ate lunch, after a fashion. And then Fred redeemed himself. "Why don't I just set up the tent and we'll call it a day," he said. That statement showed me that the man had not completely succumbed to wilderness hysteria. It was the sane thing to do, disregarding the fact that it was still only midday.

Crawling in out of the rain felt good, even though everything we owned was in various stages of wetness ranging from thoroughly damp to terminally soggy.

We slept. That felt good, too, until we woke up in a sauna. The sun had come out and evidently decided that we'd retain more vitamins if we were steamed instead of fried or boiled. We rolled out of the tent and looked around. It was still a bit windy, but, heck, it was always windy. We packed up and took off again carrying several extra pounds of water stowed away in the fibers of our moist gear. Immediately, the wind came at us from a different angle—directly into our faces. We fought our way across a couple of small bays. Forty-five minutes and about a mile and a half later, we finally did give it up for the day. It was only 2:30, and Fred felt quite put out by it all. "We didn't paddle very much today," he said. "Only about five hours."

The place we chose had been used quite some time before. It actually had a long stretch of sandy beach where we could walk right down to the lake. It was so much better than having to climb down a pile of boulders or break trail through the bushes to get water for cooking and drinking. I had to hurry supper along to beat another heavy rain coming in. We cleared up everything and dived for the tent just in time.

Early the next morning, a young arctic fox came snooping around the campfire area a couple of yards from our tent opening. We could have had some beautiful shots of it if we hadn't left our wet camera bags outside the tent the night before. Another great set of photos down the drain.

*Gosh, it's been a fun day! Drizzling rain, lots of wind, waves
threatening to smash us against the rocks, and if we're really
lucky (rumble, rumble), we might get a thunderstorm soon,
probably before I get supper finished. Golly gee!*

Knee Lake was the last big one we would cross, and we
would finish it off that day. I hoped that meant we would
no longer have such boisterous wind and waves to con-
tend with. When we ran with the waves, they kept our
arms sore from trying to hold the canoe steady and stay on
course. When we paddled along the shore around the
bays, we had to struggle against either water rebounding
off the bank or incoming waves shoving us against the
rocks.

We had made our way almost to the end of Knee Lake
and were out of the worst for awhile when we saw four
log structures in a little clump across a short reach of wa-

ter. We crossed over to them and poked around. They seemed to have been part of a trading post many years ago. There was one newer building which indicated that the place had been used within the previous two or three years as a fish shipping station. We figured the fishermen brought their "hauls" there to be taken out by plane. The old buildings were made of big logs with small saplings nailed in the cracks. One building was half-filled with large chunks of frozen snow or ice with lots of leaves, mud, and other debris in it. It must have been a cold storage house of some sort.

Having a partner who is a careful map reader gave me confidence in knowing where we were at all times. Looking across a large body of water at a distant wall of trees is confusing even to experts. It was only when one group of trees appeared to move slowly away from another group that we could distinguish islands and points from the mainland as we approached them on the water. Even then, there was no way to be absolutely sure what kind of land formation was emerging until we could see the sky meeting the water on one or both sides of it. If we had gone too far to one side or the other of the wrong group of trees, it could have meant a lot of extra paddling to correct the error.

The diminished food supply had enabled us to consolidate several of our bags. We had eaten our way down to double portages instead of triple. That was good, because the next part of the river was a portage lover's paradise. Between Knee Lake and Swampy Lake, the short segment of the Hayes River had been called Little Jack River in the old days. It contained numerous rapids around which we had to carry everything.

In one open stretch, we saw bubbles ahead. The small patch of rough water was moving toward us. In a few seconds, we could see shiny black heads and whiskered snouts bobbing up and down. A family of five otters began *schnuff-schnuff*ing loudly at us, trying to find out what had invaded their world. They all disappeared a few feet in front of the boat, just as I focused my camera, of course. We knew we were still being inspected from down under, but they never gave me a second chance at a snapshot.

We stopped at one place to look over an empty trapper's cabin made of small logs. The builder had used sod on the roof, and weeds were growing from it. The roof and floor were made of small logs split with a chain saw. The cabin was only about six feet high in the middle. A petroleum drum served as a stove, and there were crude bench-like structures built next to the wall. We guessed they were bed frames.

We camped on Swampy Lake. It didn't seem any swampier than many of the other lakes, but it was noisier. Gulls, terns, crows, and birds we had never met before gathered together for a great union meeting on a small rock island just off-shore from our campsite. For a long time after we went to bed, they aired their complaints—screeching, croaking, and rasping about all kinds of things. I didn't much like the tone of their voices. I had a feeling they might be plotting against us.

The next unusual event worthy of note was a gentle, sunny day with the wind to our backs. We even made it into the tent that evening before we felt the familiar sprinkles of rain. We camped near one of the more obvious portages. It was only a few paces across and consisted mainly of a huge rock point. The end of it was overflowing with water crashing down through boulders and over ledges. We had a nice view of a small waterfall we had just walked around. The white water tumbled over its ledge the full width of the river.

We rested pretty well. The only fly in my sleeping potion was my anticipation of the rapids ahead. I consoled myself, "Surely we can make it. We've come all this way and learned so much."

I had no idea that the last rapids would be the worst.

LARGE LAKES

The last of the big ones
    Kicked up quite a fuss;
Cold rain and waves
    Both ganged up on us.

The wind leaned against us
    While we crossed Knee Lake.
We nearly wore out;
    We needed a break.

We stopped for some lunch
    On a nice grassy shore.
The rain never quit;
    It continued to pour.

Sooner than usual,
    We parked for the night;
Our minds and our bodies
    Were tired of the fight.

A shy arctic fox,
    Log buildings of old,
A magnetic island;
    These memories we hold.

Forty miles later
    And nearly two days,
We finished the lake:
    TENACITY PAYS!

Last Rapids

The old Hayes hadn't been very kind to us for several days. During the previous 150 miles or so, it had toyed with our emotions by concealing rocks just beneath the surface of the water. Its banks had been so swampy or steep that, even though we were already exhausted, we'd had to paddle extra hours just to locate a place big enough to plant a tent.

The river had also threatened us with more of its rapids. Several times we were confronted with a mirage that looked like smooth water. The only hint to the contrary was an optical illusion in the form of a black line running straight across the river a short distance in front of us. There was no sound of rushing water, no foam, no riffles—just a long stretch of quiet water. We would paddle toward the innocent-looking "line," and suddenly I would be peering over a three-foot drop with the river laughing hysterically up at me from below. We had to do some powerful back-paddling a couple of times. Judging from the fact that we didn't go over any of these or even take on water, we must have gleaned a tiny bit of expertise from the hundreds of miles we had traveled. On the other hand, maybe it was just luck.

Then the great viper would spread itself out to a half mile in width. We spent precious time and energy searching from one side to the other and from one island to the next for a decent way around the rough water. Most of the time there was no decent way to be found. We had to create our own. Deadfalls snagged shirts and pants, muskeg sucked at boots, and immense squadrons of mosquitoes zeroed in and dived on any unprotected areas of skin. And our friends back home were going to ask, "Didja have fun on your trip?'

We came to what the map promised was the "Last Rapids." I just hoped the expression was merely a description of a few rocks in the river and not a prophecy about the end of my paddling career. This concern over semantics was brought on by something Fred had said a few days earlier about having to portage across a rock island in the middle of the falls. I was tired of worrying about the rapids and had been looking forward to being done with them. That comment drove my mind back into its usual flurry of picturing how it was going to be. I resumed my habit of coaching myself: "Now, you know how things you worry about always turn out to be insignificant. It'll be just like all the others—a piece of cake!"

After we had worked our way across the river and back again in search of yet another obscured portage, Fred finally saw the small rock island. We moved back upriver against a strong current in order to get in position for the approach. Tons of water churned past huge boulders and crashed over ledges on either side of the island. My stomach did its own churning when I realized that I had lied to myself. If any pieces of cake were to be involved at all, they would be our "just desserts" for coming on this trip in the first place!

We headed the canoe down-river and began the descent. The current was splitting at the very place where we had to make our landing. I was thankful for the adrenalin pumping through my system because most of the other fluids in my body had turned to tapioca. As we dashed toward the goal, I perused several choice contact points. The canoe, however, selected for itself a quaint trio of rocks which consisted of a small squarish boulder, a slippery round one the size of a bushel basket, and an odd little pointy thing that resembled a miniature iceberg. The iceberg was located on the other side of a three-foot-wide stream of shallow water flowing across a rock slab. We came close enough to grab the rocks and stop the canoe. There a comment from my partner convinced me that his excessive adrenalin must have caused severe brain damage. He suggested that I step out onto the closest of the three rocks, with the icy water ripping past as if it would sweep away the whole island.

Upon finishing my five-second evaluation of his diminishing mental capacity, I was amazed to find myself in a squat position perched on the bushel basket. My white-knuckled hands were still clamped to the starboard gunwale of the canoe. My feet were slipping out from under me, one at a time and sometimes in unison. In the meantime, Fred had attempted to step onto the small squarish rock at the rear.

Watching my own dancing feet slip-sliding away did not boost my spirits, and the foaming water thundering over the large boulders to my right was truly depressing. My mind was diverted from those small problems, however, by a few anxious words from the stern: "You'll have to hop onto that other rock up there and grab the bow. I can't hold this end. The current is pushing against the sides of the canoe, and it's gonna come around."

My brain was thoroughly occupied with my gross motor functions at that time and was a little slow to take in the information. When I turned toward the source of the words, I noticed the sun sparkling on the expanse of swift water, ever widening, between the stern of the canoe and the rock that was formerly my partner's foothold. I saw two arms and one leg being stretched farther and farther across this expanse. These three limbs were magically attached to the small squarish rock, though the remaining leg and the body to which they belonged were precariously perched in the canoe. For a split second, I was overcome with a morbid curiosity as to the combined tensile strength of these three human appendages. But Fred's poignant message finally took effect, and I was jerked back to reality by his coda to the original refrain: "I'm losing my grip!"

I hastily analyzed the two alternatives from which I would have to choose if I decided *not* to leap across the three feet of rushing water in hopes of landing on the pointy little iceberg. The first alternative was to let go of the canoe and wave a fond farewell to Fred as he rapidly approached his brief but exciting trip through the boulders. A second and even less appealing choice was to join my partner in the canoe for some first-hand experience in going over the seven-foot falls.

After all, we had reported our intended route to the Royal Canadian Mounted Police and had already made contact with them twice. They would at least know which half of the province to search. Surely within a decade or two, they would find shreds of clothing, a Swiss army knife, and a few other things that would provide positive identification, such as my tin flute or a canvass hiking shoe with a hole burned in the toe from being dried out too near the campfire. I was sure they would never find my little journal with all my careful notes or the tapes on which we had recorded our "scientific" observations or the camera and exposed film we had so carefully kept water-proofed. But at least, the family could go ahead and settle the estate. Of course, *most* of the estate would already be settled—in the bottom of the Hayes River.

The moment had arrived. Having assessed the grim alternatives as thoroughly as I could in the split second that remained, I decided to avoid both and jump for the iceberg. I leaped and landed. My feet regularly entangle themselves in the telephone cord at home and send me sprawling, but a miracle took place—they stayed under me! My hands gripped the point of the bow. And then, as if we were doing a carefully timed stunt scene for a movie, Fred released his grip on the squarish rock. The stern of the canoe swung out into the current and started around. I waited until just the right moment and then began pulling the bow up into the stream over which I had just jumped. A few more inches, and it was secure!

Fred took a deep breath and sang out a cheerful, "Atta Girl!" Then he hopped out and grabbed a gear bag, happily in his element once more.

I began breathing again. When enough oxygen had reached my brain to reactivate it, I got out and slowly carried my bag across the small island. Then I just rested for awhile. My heart eventually returned from its trip to my throat. I sat on a rock bluff above the put-in, looking to the left at the water pouring over the rocky ledges and to the right at white foam churning over boulders. I thought about how lucky I was to have bones that were all con-nected to each other and skin that covered them ade-quately from stem to stern. I was hoping I could keep them that way for the remaining 150 miles or so. How thoroughly I succeeded would be the criteria for shaping my answer to the inevitable question: "Didja have fun on your trip?"

RUNNING THE RIVER

What's next for us, Old River?
　　More rapids, rocks, or rain?
Go on and dish it out;
　　We're ready for the pain.

You're bent on getting wider;
　　You can't scare us away.
NAH! We'll just keep on goin'
　　Between your banks of clay.

We'll float through smaller rapids,
　　And walk around the rest.
You wanna see persistence?
　　Watch us pursue our quest.

Just keep the current coming,
　　And push us right along;
For when you think you've got us,
　　We'll show you that you're wrong!

Hills

At last, we were done carrying everything around water that was too fast to paddle. Praise the Lord! For me, the rapids had been the most harrowing of our experiences. According to some of the books I've read, I should have felt a real rush when I was being whisked over rocks and around boulders the size of a Volkswagen. But by the time we hit the calm water at the end of them, the main thrill for this chick (short for "chicken heart") was finding herself still in the canoe with paddle in hand.

Then there had been the stress of seeking out the portage trails. Fred did the seeking out while I endured the stress of waiting. His stress was physical; mine, mental. I was terribly insecure about being smaller than the living things lurking nearby. Actually, I felt no real threat from the lurking. Lurking was okay. It was the thought of more aggressive pursuits that intimidated me. There were times I'd have offered to trade roles with Fred, but I was afraid he'd accept. If I'd had to find the trails, we would still be there. Once we were in the throes of portaging, there was no way I could keep up with the Wilderness Machine. I strove earnestly to stay close enough to make a few fleeting appearances so that I would not be entirely forgotten.

But now all of that was behind us. The wide old Hayes

stretched out before us—so shallow at times we had to be careful not to run aground or bump a stray boulder just below the surface of the water. Sometimes we would hear rushing water ahead, and I would strain my eyes to see if the river was going to do it to us one more time. But the noise would be coming from water flowing around a small stick or over a tame rock. From then on, I could forget about rapids and focus on the "P" word. Polar bears were supposed to be unpredictable and territorial. I was becoming more uneasy by the hour about how these traits would affect my relationship with one of them if it should try to become acquainted with me.

We came to a patch of tall grass growing up from a submerged sand bar in a bend of the river. We were pleasantly surprised to see a cow moose and her knobby-headed son having some tender grass roots for lunch. Standing in water up to their bellies, they stopped and stared at us. Their large ears flopped noisily when they tried to shake off the flies. They watched us closely but made no effort to leave as we eased up on the opposite side of the grass. We were able to get our cameras out, for a change, and shoot several frames before they finally decided they were running the risk of becoming a picture on a calendar. Then they moved away into deeper water on the other side of the river. I felt a twinge of guilt. Not only had we interrupted them at mealtime, but we had also made them suspicious of their favorite dining establishment.

In addition to beluga whales, polar bears, and seals, the Hudson Bay area is famous for its wild goose population. We startled a gaggle of geese (I've always wanted to use that phrase) in the last section of the river. The ten to fifteen geese began to scatter when they saw us. Some swam across the river, others hurried up the side of the bank.

They must have been going through a molting or breeding season because they acted sluggish and didn't seem to be able to fly. One that had been in the grass on the bank was so overwhelmed by our approach that it waddled out into the water and tore across the river in front of us. It flailed its wings in an attempt to become airborne, but all it could do was splash along the surface of the water paddling with its feet.

The swift current hurried us on downstream past Brassy Hills. These were strange mounds sticking up against the sky in a land that has no other such configurations for several hundred miles. They have surely been used often through the years as look-out points. In earlier days, the Hayes River along that area was called Hill River because of these mounds. In some stretches, yellow clay riverbanks rose nearly fifty feet straight up.

We felt like seasoned wilderness travelers by then. We had learned to overcome hundreds of minor problems in our camping techniques. Still, we kept that foolish dream alive in our hearts that someday we might find a "nice" campsite. We began casual scanning early that day while the weak sun was still trying to show through the clouds. As usual, the temperature dropped to an uncomfortable range late in the afternoon. Our campsite requirements began to diminish until finally, upon the arrival of a cold misty rain, the only prerequisite to putting our tent down was that our feet wouldn't sink into the mud more than just ankle deep.

On the inside of a wide bend, Fred saw a level area that looked open enough. There were even a few pine trees sheltering the little haven. Lovely! It had only a couple of minor drawbacks. It was at least thirty feet above our heads, and the soft clay bank was exposed more than usual. There were, however, a couple of size-twelve flat rocks within stepping-out distance of the river so that we were able to disembark without being submerged nostril-deep in the yellow cookie dough. Fred began vigorously carrying gear to and fro, of course. It wasn't until the third trip back to the canoe that he slipped off the rocks. He managed to climb out of the quagmire all by himself and went plodding right on up the bank to make camp. He stepped quickly to avoid becoming permanently planted. The mud sucked at his boots, making a kind of "*schlook-splat*" sound each time he plunged a foot into it.

In the meantime, I was slopping up and down searching for two or three rocks large enough to hold my small grill over an anemic little fire. The initial placement of the food crematorium turned into a vicious struggle against gravity. I began by carving a niche out of the mud bank. It was just level enough so that the smoldering sticks probably wouldn't roll down into the river before they could be consumed by fire. These sticks were a necessary part of the sacrificial rite we laughingly called "Suppertime" in those days. Maintaining my equilibrium on the steep bank was a monumental task. Above and beyond that, I was faced with the problem of making the little grill level enough so that the old black coffee pot wouldn't topple off. I found myself talking to bowls and cups, pleading with them to "stay" while I poured boiling food and drink into them. It was quite a trick to keep them from tipping over and rolling down the riverbank, with or without the smoldering sticks and/or the old black coffee pot.

By sheer perseverance and extraordinary lung power, I had coaxed a damp little blaze out of some waterlogged sticks. I had used up more matches and fire starter cubes than on any other fire I had built, ever! The mist had developed into a full-fledged drizzle, nasty and cold. I became desperate to find a way to shelter the weak flame.

Rain, mud, campfire on a hillside, cold, tired.
This is as near as I can come to a smile for the camera.

Hoisting a tarp above this bare acre of mud would have been nearly impossible. I tried putting a few pieces of wood across the fire to protect it for awhile. I dared not let it go out!

Across several yards of cookie dough, on the level bank high above, my beaverish partner was building our nest. I sent an appeal skyward, "Fred, would you bring a couple of sticks of firewood when you come down this way?"

"Huh?" came the usual response. Typically, there was no let-up in the thrashing and rustling that had drowned out my first rendition of the request. A loud repetition evoked a matter-of- fact, "I'm not comin' down that way."

I had been blowing and puffing myself red in the face on that sick little spark of fire, which was being further threatened by the increasing rain. I was incensed at my fellow camper for being so callous in my time of need. I wanted to scream, "Would you just bring some wood down here! This stupid fire won't burn! It's raining! I'm tired! Nothing's level! I can't stand up! It's *raining!* Everything's muddy and slick! I'm freezing! IT'S RAINING! And . . . I *need* you!"

But instead, I slorped up the hill, battered my way through the bushes, and found three only slightly damp pieces of deadfall. I gathered them in my arms and stalked past *him* to my smoldering sticks. (The photo Fred snapped at that moment unfortunately conveyed my mood extremely well.)

But the fire survived the rain, the slope, and my anger. In a little while, when he felt it was safe enough to come within an arm's length of me, Fred wandered down to check out the smell faintly resembling food cooking. We both stood around,trying to keep our shortest legs on the high side of the bank, and ate our humble fare. Eventually, we spoke one or two words which broke the ice a bit. They were poignant and thought-provoking:

"Got any more stew?" Fred asked.

"Yeah."

"You want it?"

"No," I said.

"Here, take part of it."

"I said I don't want it."

"You need it for the energy. You're getting too skinny."

"(Sigh.) If I eat four bites of it, will you leave me alone?"

"I love you," he said.

"I know."

Cleanup was a real joy. There's probably still some stew on the pot we used that night. Then, like a scene from a television commercial produced by someone who has never camped out in his entire life, the two of us, hand in hand, romantically slopped through the muck and drizzle to the attic bedroom. It was a real luxury to crawl inside the tent out of the soggy air. We stripped off a few outer layers of damp garments and zipped ourselves into the dry sleeping bags.

I was about to drift off when I heard Fred mumble, "Um-m-m! It just doesn't get any better than this!"

I moved my arm. My hand accidentally landed on his ribs, right on the most ticklish spot.

DIFFERENCES

Husband Fred and his Fearful Fraulein
    Went out in a boat one day.
They had decided to go on a trip,
    Taking the wilderness way.

Bold and brave was Joyce's mate,
    And though she loved him much,
She wasn't quite ready to meet her Maker
    By starving, drowning, or such.

He seemed to be able to go on forever,
    But she seemed ready to quit.
How in the Sam Hill they'd ever succeed
    Was a puzzle, they had to admit.

She could take credit for several things:
    She handled the mud and the sweat,
Mosquito bites, and bathrooms outdoors,
    Days that were cold and wet.

Slow and awkward at moving, however,
    She crawled when he was flying.
He'd be annoyed with her slowness, and yet,
    He really could see she was trying.

She'd watch him battle his way through the bush
    As if he were under attack,
Charging along with canoe on his head
    And a forty-pound pack on his back!

He'd paddle ferociously on and on,
    A voyageur's speed to maintain.
Weak and tired and usually sore,
    She rested again and again.

The balance was often a bit lopsided
  Between his "fast" and her "slow."
But down that river they went together
  Where some had dared not go.

Their speed never did quite measure up
  To Fred's utmost desiring,
But Joyce stood firm in her rationale:
  She'd kept him from expiring!

They rounded many a riverbend,
  Unsure of what they'd find.
And they confirmed, beyond a doubt:
    *FORE*sight is poorer than *HIND*-.

The hat.

Last Camp

Wider is better? Well, maybe. As we neared the Bay, the old Hayes became a broad expanse of smooth water. In spite of its serene appearance, we had to stay alert for shallow gravelly spots. The current helped push us along at a pretty good clip, but occasionally the river bed rose up and rasped against the bottom of the canoe. It was like riding in a car that had wet brakes that would "grab." Then there was the wind. We'd roll right along with the swift current, paddle around a wide bend, and suddenly the wind would slap us in the face. It would continue to flog us until we reached another bend, miles away, that had high banks on the windward side.

The closer we got to the Bay, the colder the air became. I added layer upon layer of clothing as the hours went by. Finally, I had put on everything I could possibly wear and still move my arms. I even pulled one of the camping mattresses over my lap. My feet were getting numb in spite of heavy wool socks *and* cotton socks inside my Maine hunting boots. The bow of the canoe didn't allow much room for leg movement to help increase blood circulation. When I would quit paddling even for a few minutes, I'd begin to get cold. If we stopped on the bank for any kind of break, I was compelled by the chill to expedite as much as possible the fulfillment of the objectives of our landing. In other words, it was so blasted cold that I had to get it done fast and keep moving or I'd have frozen off several important body parts!

We managed about fifty-five miles, as nearly as we could figure it. We fought the wind and froze in the damp air all day long, but things cleared up slightly just as we were ready to quit for the day. Our last camp of the trip was on an open point with a wide sandy beach on each side. It was the most scenic area we had come upon for awhile. The bugs weren't even bad. My first inclination was to be thrilled with it. So many things had gone wrong with our previous camps, however, that I chose to remain safely skeptical. I did love the beach, though, and I thought Fred was just being foolish and finicky when he grumbled about sand getting into everything. (A couple of months later back at home, he informed me that the Optimus II stove wouldn't work because of all the grit that had lodged in places where air and fuel had formerly been able to move about freely.)

Our camp was on a point formed by the junction of the God's River and the Hayes. The older Indians had called the God's River the Shamattawa. We had a nice view of both rivers for a couple of miles in either direction. It is believed that Pierre Esprit Radisson, one of the leading fur traders and supposedly the first white man to ascend the Hayes River, met with a group of Indians there in 1685 to talk them into bringing their furs all the way to York Factory to trade with the Hudson's Bay Company.

Also, at that junction, maybe even on the very spot

where our tent rested, Eric Severeid and his friend Walter C. Port had camped fifty-five years before. Severeid has distinguished himself in several fields of journalism, but he is probably best-known for being a television newscaster on CBS for a number of years. He and Walt made a canoe journey all the way from Minneapolis to York Factory just after they graduated from high school. The articles that they wrote and sent back to the newspapers while they were on the trip helped launch his career as a journalist. Severeid gives an interesting account of the York Factory journey in his book *Canoeing with the Cree*.

Except for the cold wind, the campsite was a bit above average for this trip. The meal preparations weren't even as difficult as they had been at some of my earlier kitchens on the river. In fact, it seemed an appropriate time to do one more pot of beans. I was not destined to be able to relax completely. We had lived on that spot for less than an hour when we came upon some kind of unusual animal tracks in the sand. Those, I could handle. It was the fresh bear print on the other side of the point that pushed the old adrenalin up again. Thoughts of ordinary brown bears nearby had always caused a quickened heart rate, but now, thoughts of white bears caused the juices to soar.

Since the beginning of the trip, I had nursed a nagging little fear instigated by writers whose purpose in life evidently was to instill a fear of polar bears into the hearts of campers. I had read pamphlets, encyclopedias, and magazine articles about these bears. The composite of information was not encouraging. Certain phrases sent a chill through my system: "Extremely territorial, unpredictable, large, weighing over 700 pounds, at times." I was hoping the descriptions were exaggerated. The worst one of all was "Polar bear *breeding* grounds on Hudson Bay!"

I had survived day to day, hour to hour by soliciting

Fred's promise of better things ahead. I used a generic plea that covered several areas. I would say, "Will this (a) rapids, (b) lake, (c) portage, or (d) upriver stretch, be as bad as (a) The Minago River, (b) Knee Lake, (c) the rock point, (d) the muskeg trail, or (e) the road?"

Usually the reply from my relatively kind-hearted partner was, "No, it won't be as bad." But I had learned during the preceding weeks that words of comfort are cheap. Not that I didn't believe him. It was just that, when he really wasn't sure himself, he was willing to fake security in order to keep me from giving up and crawling in the tent to hibernate forever.

The food was unpacked, cooked, eaten, and the remains cleared away. Dusk and mosquitoes arrived simultaneously. That fact alone behooved us to turn in at the first hint of darkness. Lying in the tent, I began to drift off to sleep thinking about a daydream Fred had told me he used to have as a boy. He said he could imagine himself performing some kind of spectacular feat, such as making the final tie-breaking point in a basketball tournament. Crowds were cheering and the music was playing just for him. He called it "hearing trumpets." I wondered if we were close enough to York Factory for the trumpets to begin. I felt pretty good about our chances of making it the rest of the way, but until the old supply depot was actually in sight, I was a bit superstitious about claiming victory. Too many things could still happen.

Then I let my thoughts slip dangerously near to the polar bear breeding grounds. I wondered how many polar bears might be there. I could just imagine . . . . Well, I didn't want to think any further on that subject! I gave it up for the night.

C-C-COLD C-C-CANOEING

N-N-Noses are red;
F-F-Fingers are blue;
T-T-Toes are all frozen;
Kn-Kn-Knees are numb, too!

Yes!

A mist-covered river greeted us at daybreak on that last cold morning. We packed up and started out, knowing we would be stopping soon for something hot to eat and drink. The wind was down, but we were sure the early morning calm wouldn't last long. The fog lifted slowly but a fine rain fell from the familiar lead-gray sky. Our breath turned to vapor when it hit the cold air.

We finally found a spot along the high muddy bank where the small stones were close enough together to keep our feet from sinking into the sticky yellow mud. A dead tree left on the bank by high waters furnished fuel for a fire. I was hoping to revive parts of my body that were temporarily out of service. I encouraged my circulatory system to "reach out and touch *numb* ones." The hot cereal, tea, and soup were the best we'd ever tasted, and the warmth they provided for our hands made them worth double coupons.

We moved on. Standing still just made us colder, if that was possible. The sun finally put in an appearance, but it was feeble, as usual. It bolstered our spirits a bit but warmed the air very little. The river grew increasingly wider the closer it came to Hudson Bay. During the next several hours, I contemplated what effect the tide would have on our progress when we made our final approach to the Bay. I had read that the tidewaters come inland on the Hayes River for about seven miles and the water level rises twelve feet with the tide. Somehow I had gotten it into my head that there was suddenly going to be a backwash of water coming at us when the tide rolled in. So I was desperately hoping the tide would be on its way out when we were heading down those last few miles.

Another uncertainty was the whereabouts of the large white bears. I fervently hoped they would just go ahead and have a good time doing whatever it was they liked to do on their summer vacation so that we could finish ours. I really put my back into it on that last stretch in order to get to York Factory in a hurry. I personally did not intend to stay overnight on a riverbank where I might cramp the style of an animal the size of a pickup truck.

*During a lunch break, Fred is showing me
that we are getting close to Hudson Bay.*

At the start of the trip, paddling from Cumberland House to The Pas had seemed like an insurmountable task. At the finish of the trip, we started clicking off those last sixty miles with efficiency and strength I wouldn't have thought possible. The river widened more and more. I was encouraged when I began to see the large islands Fred had pointed out on the map just a few inches from York Factory.

An aluminum canoe, bashed in and bent double, lay on the beach at the head of one of the islands. Could it have wiped out in the last rapids? That was highly unlikely because they were a hundred miles or so back upriver. It had probably been tied up at one of the trapper's camps and had been torn loose when the spring thaw started the ice moving downriver toward the Bay. We had seen the scars made by chunks of ice grinding against the trees high up on the riverbanks. Enormous rocks had been turned over and wrenched loose. The noise must have been tremendous.

I couldn't be satisfied until I had looked under the smashed canoe to see if the owner (or the remains thereof) might be nearby. I was relieved to find nothing. I certainly didn't need a pile of bleached bones to cast a darker shadow on my morale. I can't imagine why I thought anyone would or even could stay in a wrecked canoe until it washed ashore.

We put the islands behind us and came to a place where the river was so wide we could hardly see the trees on the other side. Fred said, "Do you see that open part up ahead where the water and the sky meet?" He pointed to an area just off the right of the bow. "That's the Bay!"

It won't be long now! I thought. *I could SWIM from here, if I had to.* My eyes had been searching the left side of the river for over an hour. About 6:30 P.M., I spotted something on top of the high steep bank. I said, "Oh, *look!*" So far up ahead that it was barely visible stood a pole flying a red flag.

"That's it!" Fred confirmed.

The answer to my prayers! I eased up on my paddling and relaxed a little. I just wanted to let the elation soak in. I wouldn't even have had to swim that last quarter of a mile. I could have walked across the water!

Then a small plane circled high over the flagpole and disappeared into the distant skies. My heart quivered. Uneasiness began to cloud my glorious moment. I had heard that the old factory was deserted except for a keeper who stayed there most of the time. Watching that plane fly off, I was trying hard not to believe that the only living soul within 100 miles was leaving. Maybe the keeper had locked up everything and was departing for the weekend to go

York Factory

home to be with the family or something. After all, it wasn't as if we had made an appointment. I began to think I might still have to camp out next door to the polar bear breeding grounds of the North Country. Not only that, but the person contained in that plane might be the only one who could put us in touch with the outside world so that we could get home.

As we drifted closer, we could see that the flag bore a miniature Union Jack in one corner. The letters H.B.C. were in the lower edge of the field. Next, we saw a sign that read YORK FACTORY, PARKS CANADA. We had arrived at what was once the largest and most important trading post of Hudson's Bay Company for at least two centuries. We were too close to the high bank to be able to see the old depot on top of it. We paddled the canoe up to a floating dock. Fred got out and began to climb the long set of wooden steps built up the side of the muddy bank. Typically, I took longer to get out and start the flight of stairs, so I was a short distance behind him when he reached the top. I heard another voice. Relief! At least one other person was there! When I cleared the last step, I saw Fred talking to a young man named Dave, who turned out to be an employee of Parks Canada.

Then I saw the big square depot, standing alone against the sky. Magnificent! I wanted to run right over to it, but it seemed terribly far away when I realized how tired I was. In a few minutes, Lily McAuley, a Parks Canada interpreter, came down the long boardwalk from the small living quarters. Her fiancé, Wilf Van Steelandt, appeared shortly afterwards. They knew exactly how to welcome two tired, hungry canoeists. They took us to the small metal building where they were staying while Lily did her two-week stint as historical interpreter for the old factory. She served us a small lunch of camembert cheese, homemade bread, and even orange brandy—in real glasses. After days of squatting on sloping riverbanks chewing our way through beef stew and chili-mac, her meal was a royal feast!

No roads into that place! And this time, there were no cars, either. It was far too rugged. It seemed like the edge of the world. I certainly hadn't expected eight people to be staying there. Five of the eight were John Hatley and a crew of four, including two of his sons. Hatley ran a goose hunting lodge comprised of a main building and three cabins.

The areas around all of the buildings had been cleared and mowed as far out as the roughness and swampiness would permit. But there was only a narrow trail through the tall grass and willows between the old factory and the new lodge area. "A boardwalk, built a year after we were there, now connects these two areas."

On the whole point of land reaching out into the Bay, only two buildings remained where there had once been fifty or more structures. A small white frame library building stood just to the rear of the huge depot. We found out later that it was built in the early part of the twentieth century. The old three-story landmark was in the shape of an open square with a grassy area in the center crisscrossed by a boardwalk leading to opposing doors. The layout was designed for the most efficient use of space and energy.

"A monstrous blot on a swampy spot with a partial view of the frozen sea!" was what Robert Ballantyne said about York Factory in *Hudson Bay*. He was a fur trader stationed there in 1843. The weather, insects, and isolation from loved ones must have driven more than one former inhabitant into deep depression. Yet, there was a lingering spirit of industry and hints of an active social life complete with parties. I was caught up in the aura. I wanted to see

the graffiti on the walls of the large central area of the depot. Scratched into the wood are names, dates, heights and
weights of some of the people who lived and worked there.
I wanted to stand by the fur press and imagine the preparations that were necessary for shipping the pelts to Eu-
rope. I had read about the round marks left permanently
on the wooden floor by the storage kegs. In the later years,
from around 1930 on, there had been a leather-working
room. One of the artifacts still in the depot is part of a
printing press possibly used to print religious literature.

From the lookout turret on top of the old building,
many anxious watchers of long ago looked out over Hudson Bay and wondered if the ship would come in that day.
The yearly arrival was scheduled for the end of July. The
York Factory employees would hurry to get the furs ready
so that the ship could get away by September 1. Staying
too long meant being blocked in by ice on the Bay.

The interpreter wouldn't take us to the old building
then because there wouldn't have been enough time to see
all of it before nightfall, but she promised a thorough tour
the next morning. I had a feeling that it was going to be
worth almost all the trouble it had taken to get there.

Most of that trouble had really existed only in my
mind. When I reflected on my concern about the tide
washing us back upstream, I felt foolish. I hadn't spent
much time near an ocean, but I had seen a tide or two
come in. It was like watching the minute hand on a small
clock. The movement was imperceptible. The only thing
the incoming tide could have done to us would have been
to deaden our swift current. But, as usual, my careful
planning for the worst wasn't even necessary because we
went down the river with the outgoing tide anyhow. I
wanted to steep myself in the "past," dream old dreams,
hobnob with voyageurs. But I was tired—twelve hours

and sixty miles tired. Hot water, carried in buckets by the boys who worked at the lodge, made an unbelievably luxurious sponge bath. The beds felt even better.

Rapids, wind, electrical storms, impossible portages, yucky food, desperation campsites, dwindling good humor. Was it worth all the trouble! YES!

HEARING TRUMPETS

A swatch of red hung from a pole
   Atop that bank of clay.
We had arrived at rainbow's end;
   There it was—the Bay!

We climbed the bank for our first look
   At what we'd come to see:
One big square building standing proud
   Where many used to be.

Its walls and turret, empty now,
   Preserve for those who care,
Reminders of a style of life
   With strength and courage rare.

We joined the ranks of voyageurs
   Who journeyed by canoe.
A tiny glimpse was all we saw
   Of hardships they lived through.

A lesson in humility,
   We learned from our long trip.
A cold and lonely life they gave,
   To furs and trading ships.

A trumpet fanfare far away,
   Heard only by our ears,
Echoed triumph through the ages:
   Heroes conquering fears.

York Factory

The sun rose over Hudson Bay. I missed it. I was asleep. Fred said that he had awakened in the night and couldn't understand the square of light suspended in the darkness. It was the faint light of the Northern sky showing through the window in the cabin. I, on the other hand, slept soundly after reassuring myself several times during the wee hours that the bed was neither riding on waves nor sinking into muskeg.

Thoughts of polar bears appearing suddenly along the bank or rising up out of the water had driven me down the last twenty-five miles of the river so hard that even my well-conditioned shoulders were sore that morning. However, at York Factory, with everyone else (and their guns) there, it would have been perfectly all right with me if a polar bear had put in an appearance. In fact, the day before we had arrived, one had come up in the water next to the dock. Because the big white bears are so unpredictable, the guns are carried mainly to scare them off if they suddenly come too close.

The rest of the day's events were at least equal to the

sunrise we had missed, especially the two-hour tour of the old supply depot. After breakfast at the lodge, Lily and Wilf took us on a venture into the nineteenth century fur trade. What follows is a brief summary of Lily's interpretation:

The area near the Hayes and Nelson Rivers was settled 100 years before any other area along the bottom part of Hudson Bay. York Factory was important historically, Lily told us, because it kept changing roles as time dictated. First, it was the most important fur trading post. It had more fur returns than all the other posts put together at any given time. In 1774, when Cumberland House was established, it also became a supplier to the interior. The French would take it over and give it a name such as Ft. Bourbon. The English would reclaim it and call it Ft. York. At one time they even called it New York. The French and English stole their toy from each other three times between 1694 and 1713. When the area was between ownerships and actually belonged to no one, the Indians would move in en masse and strip all the lead roofing to make shot for their guns.

Lily picked up a piece of an old clay smoking pipe. She explained that the pipes the tripmen carried were usually between twelve and eighteen inches long. As they were smoked, the part that was put in the mouth would become soft and was then broken off and thrown away. She said a whole pipe was rarely found. No one was allowed to smoke in the buildings at York Factory because of the risk of fire. There would be no way to carry enough water up the steep embankment in time to put it out. A whole building or even the whole group of buildings might go up in flames. In spite of that threat, the men would sneak a pipe now and then. The Hudson's Bay Company even tried to discourage the Indians from having individual campfires because of the danger to the buildings. The Company designated an area in which a communal fire was to be built. The Indians didn't much care for the arrangement. Each family wanted its own cooking fire.

We visited a small cemetery in which mostly Indians were buried, but there were also graves of people who had come from England, France, and Scotland to live at York Factory. We had seen well-kept graveyards at all four of the Indian reserves we had visited during our trip. Lily told us that each family has its own design for the grave markers. Some have pointed knobs on the tops of crosses. Other families have made picket fences around each grave with a carved design on the top of each picket. Several people who had come there from foreign countries have marble and limestone markers with names and dates chiseled into them. Wooden crosses, bearing only names and dates, and even rusted iron crosses marked a few of the graves.

Lily mentioned the graveyard at Cumberland House where some of her family members are buried. An interesting coincidence was that she had been born and raised at the place where we had started our journey, and we found her at the end of our journey at York Factory. Lily's father was a Scotsman and her mother was Cree. She is very proud of each ancestral heritage. She sometimes uses Cree expressions when speaking of her childhood, and she wears a Scottish kilt on special occasions. Her father made crosses of split willow for his family. It is interesting wood. The inside sometimes grows faster than the outside, causing the bark to split open and then heal itself. It makes a unique design of its own and is sometimes used for table and chair legs and other kinds of furniture.

In the fur trading days, the Indians that lived in that area were mostly Swampy Cree. Occasionally, an Eskimo or perhaps a Chipwayan would come with the sloops around the Bay. The Home Guard Indians, who served as interpreters and runners, stayed in a settlement a mile away from York Factory.

The business of exchanging furs for trade goods from across the sea had to be planned three years ahead. The people from the interior made up lists of the things they wanted. Those items were called the *indent*. The lists were sent to England in the late summer with the furs. Sometimes only half of the items on the lists would be brought back the next year. Those goods were stored in separate buildings for the winter and then were taken inland in the spring to be distributed.

Of course, all of the pelts had been extremely valuable to the *original* owners, but when they were no longer occupying the fur, the next owner graded it according to appearance. Each fur bundle coming from the interior was a deliberate mixture of low-grade pelts and valuable furs. If all of the most expensive pelts had been packed together in a canoe that turned over in the rapids or swamped on a windy lake, the loss would have been tremendous. When the fur bundles arrived at York Factory, they were quickly taken apart and repacked according to value before the ship had to leave.

The HBC had to keep a two-year supply of things on hand in case the ship didn't come in when it was expected. If it was delayed for any reason, it wouldn't be able to get into the Bay because of ice. Then it wouldn't return until the next year. A hundred miles up the coast, the Prince of Wales Port was passed by more often. The ships would go on to York Factory because of storms or ice. The people at Prince of Wales had many hard times. Sometimes they could even see the sails in the distance across the bay as the ship kept on going to York instead of stopping there.

Not only were they watching their food and other much needed supplies vanish, but also the ship was carrying away important messages from home for another whole year.

Among the buildings that had formerly stood on the grounds, there were barns, a blacksmith shop, a boat builder's house, a canoe house, an inland cargo building, an ice house, and a dog meat house. A tailor, cooper, stone mason, and physician were among the employees. The cooper was perhaps nearly as important as the doctor because of the demand for barrels to use in shipping the trade goods. A small oilcloth factory produced cloth dipped in some kind of oil until it became waterproof. Fresh vegetables and fruits were so scarce that scurvy became a serious problem. The gardens weren't very successful, probably because of poor soil and the short growing season.

In 1713, the whole settlement was located about two miles farther out on the Hayes River nearer to the coast, but there were bad problems with the ice and flooding. In 1788, Joseph Colon moved the settlement to the present location. When Captain John Franklin came there in 1819, he reported that the two-story buildings were placed in the form of a square with an octagonal court in the center.

The present structure was built on top of the foundation of "Old Octagon." In one of the ground-floor rooms, Lily showed us where the beams of the octagon were emerging after archaeologists had disturbed them five years before. She said it was because of a boiling up of the earth. The permafrost had shifted and pushed the beams upward. She called it "frost-boil." The three-story front section of the square depot was built in 1832. The remaining two-story wings and back building of the square were not finished until 1837.

One of the rooms inside York Factory.
The marks from the shelves still show on the walls.

There were problems with flooding in that area also. Ditches were dug for drainage, but because of the disturbance to the permafrost, the sides often caved in. Erosion continues to take away the land along the river frontage, at times nearly a yard per year. The permafrost is about twelve feet deep. When the frost melts along the coast, the clay oozes out and falls down to the beach below.

Workmanship on the depot was done mostly by shipbuilders and ship's carpenters. In order to allow for the constant shifting of the permafrost below, the walls of the building were not attached to the floor. When the walls would go too far out of alignment, a kind of wedge was used to correct them. In some corners, we saw huge hooks and eyes, also used for realignment purposes. The carpenters seemed to find these techniques as appropriate for constructing a large building on the frost boiling ground as they did for making sailing vessels that would "give" slightly rather than be pulled apart by wind and waves. The old depot floating on the permafrost is a credit to her builders.

Some of the supports in the building were made of trees' knees. This was the hardest wood that could be found because it was cut from the heavy bend in the roots at the base of a tree. A few of the beams had rounded edges and detailed curlicues on them. The carving was apparently an outlet for a craftsman with pride in his work. The wood did not have a treated surface but looked as rich as if it had been oiled.

The large warehouses that were part of the big square held trade goods for the interior. The fur houses and weighing rooms were all busy places in their day. Graffiti dating back to the late 1800's can be seen on the walls. Especially interesting were the notes written on the wall above the scale. Lord Simpson had been there four years and had gone to England for a furlough. He had weighed only 171 pounds before he had left York Factory. He weighed 269 after the furlough. He was later referred to as *rotund*. Lady Simpson's weight was 108 pounds.

The furs were often wet when the fur brigades brought them in after the long trip across the lakes and through the rapids. The ideal place to dry them was the courtyard inside the open square where dogs could not get to them. Also, the two boardwalks leading from opposing buildings and crossing in the center saved many steps. An additional feature of the open courtyard was that more light was admitted to the inside of the building through the extra windows facing the square. Candles, lamps, and lanterns were never allowed in the building because of the danger of fire.

The English social structure never loosened, even in that rough country. The Governor of the Day entertained his officers in full-dress uniform with all the pomp and ceremony of their military style. The young officers stayed in Bachelor's Hall, but visiting officers had other accommodations. In 1821, York Factory became a place of administration after the amalgamation of the North West Company and Hudson's Bay Company. The class structure of the Hudson's Bay Company changed. Formerly, all of the big shots had been English, but then, over half of the posts were taken over by North West Company people, many of whom were Scotsmen and French.

No longer is York Factory needed as a place of business. it has outlived its importance in the industrial world. But it is valuable as a reminder of a colorful phase of Canadian History. We are glad to see that it is being rescued from the elements by the Canadian parks system.

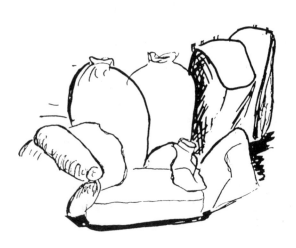

THE TORMENTORS

Oh, *sure*, Mr. Sun!
    Start shining! That's right!
Now that we're back
    In our beds every night!

Now that we're under
    A roof all day long,
Come out from hiding;
    Making those rays *strong!*

Where were you, you rascal,
    When we needed you?
You hid behind clouds
    Till the cold turned us blue!

When we tried to soak
    Some warmth from your rays,
You blistered our skin!
    We suffered for days!

And Wind, you're no better!
    You tossed us and beat us!
Then left us at dusk
    For mosquitoes to eat us!

So better luck next time!
    You'll both get a crack
At trying to outwit us,
    'Cause we're comin' back!

Back to Square One

The return trip to our car at The Pas was an adventure in itself. Our plan was to have a float plane pick us up at York Factory and fly us to Thompson, Manitoba, about 220 miles away. There we would take the train back to The Pas, where we would call Bill Allard. He would pick us up in our own car at the train station. It sounded simple enough, but the snags came in the form of expense, communication, timing, and—one of my personal favorites—*weather*.

To most people in that situation, the expense would probably have been insignificant. But the frugal Welsh blood in my veins pumped a bit faster when the price of the plane charter was quoted at seven hundred Canadian dollars. Communication to the outside world was executed on a diabolical radio phone that would cut us off if we held our eyebrows wrong. We had to coordinate the plane flight with the departure time of the train, which ran from Thompson to The Pas only on certain days of the week.

The timing was tricky. We figured the plane would have to leave Thompson just at daybreak in order for us to make our train connection, and even then it would be close.

Still a bit uneasy about the tight schedule, we crawled out of bed at 4:30 A.M. the next day to be ready for the plane. Sunlight was filtering through the fog over Hudson Bay. The Canadian flag in front of the lodge stood straight out in the stiff breeze. We ate some breakfast that Mr. Hatley and the boys had fixed, and then we all waited anxiously. The fog concerned us. We realized that planes don't do well in it, and any delay in the take-off at Thompson would mess up our timing in catching the train. But then the noise of an engine came out of the mist, and we went down by the river where the gear and the canoe had been taken.

The pilot landed the float plane and brought it as close to the beach as he could, but the tide was in and the water was choppy. He said because of the wind it would be difficult to tie up at the beach and try to load the plane on the water. He and Mr. Hatley decided it would be better for him to taxi back up to the Parks Canada dock. So everyone helped put the gear and the canoe into one of Hatley's big motorboats. We rode in style the mile and a half back upstream to the place where we had first arrived. The plane was already moored to the dock and riding the waves. We boosted the gear up and into the cabin. The pilot lashed the canoe to the struts while Lily, Wilf, and several other friends held onto the wings to steady the plane.

A few quick hugs, and then we climbed awkwardly from the heaving dock into the cabin. The pilot revved up the engine and began the short jolting take-off run. The water released the pontoons, and we were suddenly free, wheeling out over Hudson Bay partially shrouded in mist. The pilot did a fly-by of York Factory, and our friends waved up at us from the dock again.

I shivered slightly from the excitement of it all. I shivered a great deal from the cold! The weather was appropriate for the ending of the trip. One more time, I thought I might be found dead—this time stiff and blue. I wondered how they would ever extract my frozen body from that tight little compartment.

Occasionally, we were able to see through the clouds to the earth below. The winding little streams were nearly identical to the ones on which we had been traveling for over five weeks. I was amazed at the intricacy of the curves and switchbacks. We certainly hadn't taken any short cuts! We were never positive about the exact mileage we traveled. Fred measured and remeasured the distances on the maps. He came up with *about* 390 miles "as the crow flies." According to mileage quoted from other sources, he added up a total of *about* 650 miles "as the canoe floats." BUT, with his meticulous little map-measuring wheel, he traced over all the kinks in the streams, rivers, lakes and portages we covered, and he came up with *about* 850 miles. I'll buy that!

The maps had showed us where the waterways flowed and how they lay, but flat pieces of paper with lines on them could not convey the details of that panorama and the implications of those details. It was probably best that I hadn't seen quite so vivid a picture of it before we planned our trip. I was sorry I had managed only a half-dozen blurry photos during our flight. Few things in my life have ever thrilled me as much as paddling up to the York Factory dock for the first time. But our rough, windblown departure from it and the flight across the countryside was almost as exciting as our arrival.

The pilot landed on the river at Thompson. We paid our seven hundred dollars (*choke, choke*) and flung the gear and the canoe into a pickup truck. An off-duty pilot named

*Getting gear and canoe ready to put on the train
for the trip back to The Pas.*

Lyle drove us to meet the train. I remember him especially
well because he looked at me in awe. He was flabbergasted
at the idea of a forty-five-year-old woman going on a trip
with her husband into the bush.

We knew we were cutting the time close to when we
would have to catch the train. We pulled into the station,
and my heart sank. The train was pulling out. We didn't
know it then, but if we had hopped out of the truck and
shouted a bit, we could probably have stopped it. The
"Muskeg Express" caters to people in that area a great deal
more than even our school buses do in Indiana. We were
in a quandary, but after all, it wasn't as bad as the water
wall at Moose Lake or the Last Rapids. We could handle it.

Lyle suggested that we go back to the airfield and see if

his boss would let him take us to meet the train at its next stop. We ended up riding an hour and a half in the truck to Wabowden. It wasn't ideal, but I did reap some additional admiration and flattery from Lyle. Of course, I gracefully rejected his praise—well, I *thought* about rejecting it. I ate it up, is what I did! We met the train, loaded our gear and canoe into the baggage car, and then took leave of our newest friend.

The train was slow, stopping several times to pick up passengers standing beside the tracks a hundred miles out in the bush. The few occupants of the train were mainly Indian families. The children were basically well-behaved and happy but under the control of their parents. They didn't constantly try to attract the attention of everyone in the car, unlike many American children I have seen. Every thirty miles or so, two or three plain little houses stood beside the tracks. Usually at least one barefoot child with shining black eyes would be standing motionless, gazing at the passing train.

Many, many days before, on June 18, we had left The Pas in our car to go to Cumberland House where we embarked on our journey. Thirty-eight days later, we arrived at York Factory. Twelve of those days, we hadn't moved, mostly because of wind, a couple of times because of fatigue. But for twenty-six days, we had either paddled a canoe or traveled on foot. Coming back to The Pas, we would make the return trip in ten hours. We would travel by motorboat, float plane, train, and automobile—but not by canoe or on foot.

Lulled by the motion of the train, I was relaxed and happy. We had finished *The Trip of Our Lives!* It was the most difficult thing I had done in all of my forty-five years. Now I could rest on my laurels. I could convince all of my friends (at least, the ones who hadn't heard about Calvin

Rutstrum or Sigurd Olson) that I was an experienced wilderness paddler. But the people on the train would never realize that a superwoman was in their midst.

While I was still basking in the afterglow and modestly trying to blend in with the "ordinary" passengers, a handful of words spoken by my husband brought me crashing back to earth. He said, "Next summer, why don't we take about two months off and do the Seal River. It's even farther north, and when we come out at the mouth of it, we can paddle right down the coast of Hudson Bay."

As far as I was concerned, I had just won the biggest battle of my life, and there he was, wanting me to start another war! I thought about the coming months and what I was in for—the extravagant sales pitches about the wild rivers, the smooth talk about the rapids not being any worse than ones that we paddled on this trip, and that unbearable enthusiasm in his voice when he talked about the number of miles we would cover. I couldn't stand to think about it. I only hoped I could hold out for a few weeks, until this new inspiration passed. I finally gathered my wits about me. "Honey," I said, "it just doesn't get any better than *THIS!*"

WE'RE BACK! whoopee.

I thought I was ready for civilization,
Leaving behind all the backwoods frustration;

But when I returned to the paved city street,
My personal habits had grown indiscreet.

We'd had few occasions when nudity mattered.
When weather'd been warm so our teeth hadn't
    chattered,

We'd skinny-dip freely with no thought in mind
Of anyone leering at us from behind.

The bush was our bathroom, at times mighty rough.
But people on sidewalks don't go for that stuff.

Returning to town was like having jet lag;
We knew what to do, but oh, what a drag!

We'd sometimes forget to use napkin and fork,
Instead of a spoon, for our barbecued pork.

When steering the car, I couldn't stay straight.
My seatbelt forgotten, I sure tempted fate!

We couldn't get used to the nit-picky things:
The sirens, the horns, the telephone rings.

The noise of the city was raucous and cruel
Compared to the wilderness, quiet and cool.

Solitude's wasted on those who won't listen
To loons on a lake or rapids that glisten.

Blind people see more than those who won't look
At the dazzling gems in the bed of a brook.

So we'll go back home to the noise and foul air,
And continue to feel our lot is unfair.

We'll pay all our dues and work for our fee,
Till we can return and set ourselves free.

Thanks, reader—

I appreciate the time and effort you put into reading my story. I hope we "meet again."

I especially want to thank you if you are a friend or relative who encouraged me, proofread for me, listened to me, or even if you just happen to like me well enough to flatter me by reading my book.

Joyce